BUYING *the* AMERICAN DREAM

BUYING *the* AMERICAN DREAM

A strategic playbook for acquiring small businesses.

MATTHEW R. MEEHAN
and LUIGI ROSABIANCA

Archway Publishing books may be ordered through booksellers or by contacting:

Archway Publishing
1663 Liberty Drive
Bloomington, IN 47403
www.archwaypublishing.com
844-669-3957

ISBN: 978-1-6657-3646-6 (sc)
ISBN: 978-1-6657-3645-9 (hc)
ISBN: 978-1-6657-3647-3 (e)

Library of Congress Control Number: 2023900141

Print information available on the last page.

Archway Publishing rev. date: 02/15/2023

CONTENTS

ROUND 3: GROWING THE BUSINESS

INTRODUCTION

What is the American Dream? A white picket fence, 2.5 kids, a yellow lab playing in the backyard, and a healthy retirement plan from a job you dedicated the last 40+ years of your life to?

While this might have been true ten or fifteen years ago, the economic landscape has shifted dramatically. Corporate America is no more. Job security is no more. In the last two decades, three financial crises and a pandemic have exposed the fallacy of a system that is no longer designed to support this dream. We are working more now than ever before (430% more since 1950, according to the U.S. BLS), and what do we have to show for it? Meager savings, long working hours, demeaning bosses, and a chain around our necks that gives the illusion of job security but is really just a noose that's tightening year after year.

Bleak, eh? This ain't no Norman Rockwell painting.

This is the new reality.

But this doesn't have to be your story. You can decide on a different path. You can decide to do what so many others are unwilling or too afraid to do.

And how can you do that?

Through business ownership.

We believe that everyone should own some type of business. Whether it's a part-time side hustle or a full-time income stream, the best thing you can do for yourself, your family, and your future is to stop depending on corporate America or a 401(k) to provide you with the financial security you need.

But starting a business from scratch isn't for everyone. We know a majority of startups fail within the first few years, and it's a massive gamble with zero assurances that it won't send you straight to the poor house.

That's why we wrote this playbook. You don't need to be a Business Starter to be a Business Owner; it's something you can acquire. **You can, quite literally, *buy the American Dream.***

Who are we?

We spent decades on Wall Street, building teams of all sizes in multiple industries. But there came the point where we'd had enough. We got tired of working for big banks and helping the rich get richer. We recognized the potential of small business ownership and how it could transform lives, but we weren't content to sit by and watch people figure it out on their own. We wanted Main Street to have the same tools and resources as Wall Street.

It was from this desire that The Liquid Lunch Project podcast was formed. A throwback reference to the days when most business deals were sealed with a handshake and a drink, we wanted to get back to those basics. We wanted to take the conversation out of elitist board rooms and elevate the discourse in the small business industry by connecting with others on a person-to-person level.

Each week we sit down with the top leaders, visionaries, authors, CEOs, pioneers, and movers and shakers in the industry. We cover everything from physical and mental health, funding options, entrepreneurship, the gig economy, real estate, and more. Our listeners (and ourselves) have learned a lot - and several of those episodes are actually linked within this book. We also launched a wildly successful newsletter called The Weekly as an extension of The Liquid Lunch Project, which has become a must-read for those interested in keeping up with the latest news, trends, and facts in the world of finance, technology, and small business.

Through the lens of our combined real-life experiences, successes (and failures) of business ownership - and, more importantly, acquiring businesses- we have assembled this strategic playbook. It's just another way we're helping people achieve their American Dream.

A Word of Warning Before You Get Started:

We like to say that everything worth doing is on the other side of hard. This isn't a get-rich-quick Ponzi scheme or a "How to Achieve Wealth in Five Simple Steps" workbook. There are plenty of shysters lurking about the bowels of the internet who would be all too happy to exchange empty promises of easy success for the *"low, low price of $99.99."* If that's what you're looking for in this book, you will be woefully disappointed.

What we will provide, however, is straightforward, actionable, common-sense instruction that anyone, no matter their background, can take and implement immediately.

Don't be surprised if you find a few extra grey hairs during the process; it will mean work. But it also means freedom and flexibility. It means creating a life and lifestyle that you have complete control over. It means not requesting (and waiting for approval) to take time off to spend with your family. It means having a say in when you work and what you do. It means no caps on your earnings potential. It means being master of your domain or captain of your ship or whatever other types of alliteration you want to use here. It means you, **and you alone,** are in control.

Huzzah!

How to Use This Playbook:

Like most things in life, there isn't a one-size-fits-all answer. We designed this playbook to take you from Beginning to End - OR to be used as a reference guide throughout your business acquisition journey.

To keep things organized, we've divided it up into three rounds (we are The Liquid Lunch Project, after all). Within each round, we cover a range of topics, like determining the type of business you want to buy and how to spot red flags or secure funding - all the way to learning how to scale and grow down the road. We've also included some links to pertinent podcast episodes, plus free worksheets and checklists to help you along the way.

Scan the QR code or visit www.theliquidlunchproject.com/buyingtheamericandream to receive a link to access all bonus materials.

It doesn't matter HOW you use this playbook; it matters what you DO with the information.

The decision you make today - *this very moment, even* - can change the entire trajectory of your life.

Maybe you're OK with how things are.

But what about a year from now?

Five years?

How do you feel about doing what you're doing right now for the rest of your life?

If you're tired of the rat race and are ready to join others who transitioned away from "job security" to a life of freedom, flexibility, and control, consider this your down payment towards buying your own American Dream.

Now, let's get to work.

ROUND 1

Find the Business

Chapter One

WHY SHOULD YOU, OF ALL PEOPLE, BUY A BUSINESS?

THINK ABOUT IT:

"I knew that if I failed, I wouldn't regret that, but I knew the one thing I might regret is not trying."

- Jeff Bezos

So, you want to own your own business. Congrats, you're in the right place! If we were with you right now, we'd raise a toast in your honor and salute you for having the chutzpa to pursue the idea of the American Dream.

If you skipped the introduction (you know who you are), you missed our soapbox moment extolling the benefits of business ownership and why we believe it's not only life-changing but also accessible to anyone.

Yes, that means YOU.

When people dream about being business owners, they often envision starting one from the ground up. They formulate a business model, create a plan, and put in a lot of legwork and research, not to mention blood, sweat, tears, and, most of all...***money.*** But there's no guarantee of success.

In fact, 60% of small businesses will fail in their very first year. (Most people like to forget about that part.) It can be a pretty big gamble. And quite a bit of work.

We're here to tell you there's a better way.

Because what you might not realize is that there are ways to ***become a small business owner without starting from scratch.*** It is possible to purchase already-established businesses using creative financing solutions that require very little to no money upfront and can start generating income for you almost immediately.

It sounds too good to be true, right? If it's that easy and lucrative, then why isn't everyone doing it?

SIMPLE: Because not everyone has the motivation, drive, passion, or determination to make it happen. Because even though the concept itself is simple, the actual execution requires you to roll up your sleeves and put in the work.

Einstein himself said that genius is one percent inspiration, 99 percent perspiration. This book is your one percent; it will inspire you to go out and achieve your dreams and give you the tools and resources you need to make them happen. The other 99 percent? ***Well, that's all up to you.***

Excited yet?

Mindset Check: Can I Really Buy a Business?

Before we go any further, we think it's important that you stop here and do a quick check-in with yourself. If your brain is already firing off a thousand and one reasons why this could work for someone else but not for you, that's a problem. We need to shift you out of that mindset. Otherwise, everything you're about to read and learn will be discolored by self-doubt. We want you going into this with an attitude of **Yes You Can.**

We don't mean *"just think happy thoughts"* or *"sending you positive vibes"* when talking about that shift. There's a time and place for that - like a Disney movie or Vision Board. This ain't it.

We're talking about training your mind to believe that you can do more.

The fact that you picked up this book shows you've already made an important first step toward achieving your goal. You're about to embark on a path that many others dare not. You will face challenges and setbacks and do things that your friends and family might think are crazy. *You're going to have moments when you think you're crazy.* You'll want to give up a million times and return to the "security" of your 9-5.

This is all normal. And it's natural to question yourself; you'll probably do quite a bit of it. You'll wonder why you ever thought you could make this work.

It's OK to question yourself.

Just make sure you're asking yourself the RIGHT questions.

Stop asking "*why me*?" **Start asking why NOT me?**

Stop asking *what if it doesn't work*? **Start asking what if it DOES work?**

Mind over matter. Remember, if you believe you can do something, you're already halfway there.

And once you've decided that **Yes You Can**, *now you need to determine* **WHY.**

Having a **WHY** is one of the most important strategies to have in your toolbelt when working toward a goal. This probably isn't the first time you've been told this, and it probably won't be your last - but that's because it is proven to work. And who doesn't want to invest in something with a proven track record?

WHY do you want to be a small business owner?

WHY do you want to be an entrepreneur?

WHY do you want something different for your life?

Maybe you want to escape the corporate ladder. Maybe you want more control over your time to spend with family or travel. Maybe it's financial independence or a legacy to leave for your children. Maybe you want the freedom of being the CEO of your own life.

Your **WHY** can be anything, but it must be meaningful enough to push you through when times get tough. If you don't have a strong reason, you'll jump ship when the waters start to get rocky.

TAKE ACTION

Spend some time right now thinking about your **WHY.** Write it on a notecard and tape it to your bathroom mirror or computer monitor or anywhere you'll see it on a regular basis. When you have moments of panic or doubt or *"to hell with all of this"* (and you will), think back to that notecard.

Chapter Two

STARTING A BIZ VS. BUYING A BIZ

THINK ABOUT IT:

"Some people dream of success, while other people get up every morning and make it happen."

- Wayne Huizenga

So now that you've established why YOU want to own a business, let's talk about WHY you should buy a business instead of starting one.

There are four main answers to this question, but we'll start with the simplest one first:

Because it's there.

Supply and demand, baby. And right now, there's supply coming out the wazoo. Would you believe there are approximately 2.5 million small businesses available for sale, yet only 1 out of 10 will sell over 12 months? And it's not because they are tanking or hemorrhaging money, and the owners are looking to bail.

Quite the opposite, actually.

The fact is that **10,000 Baby Boomers are retiring each day**. 19% of them own a small business, and 78% of these businesses are profitable[1]. (This actually makes them the ***most profitable*** age group of small business/franchise owners.) By our calculations, that means every day, approximately 1,400 opportunities to purchase a profitable business are added to the market.

That's mind-blowing.

And there's a pretty good chance we'll never see an opportunity like this again in our lifetime.

Reason number two to consider purchasing an established business is all about **Time and Money.** Starting a new business can require a lot of both.

As we mentioned, 60% of new businesses fail within the first year. A whopping 96% fail within ten years. It can take a few years even to turn a profit, and if (or when) you can pay yourself, it will probably be a median salary ($46-$58 annually) for working over 50 hours per week.

Some food (or drink) for thought:

- *If you dream of starting your own business, can you afford not to pay yourself initially?*
- *Are you willing to invest your life savings into something that might leave you flat-broke?*
- *Could you realistically hold down a full-time job to pay the bills and devote 50+ hours a week on top of that to get your business off the ground?*

We're not saying it can't be done; we're just saying this way isn't the only way.

---

1 "Boomers in Business: 2020 Trends." Guidant Financial.

Reason number three to purchase a business is the potential for **immediate passive (and usable!) income** streams. Let's say you have a business that generates $150,000 annually, and your purchase agreement requires you to pay $50,000 a year on the loan. That leaves you with $100,000, which you can reinvest to grow that business - ***or buy or start another one.***

And finally, the **fourth reason** purchasing a business is a good investment is that **you know it works.** They already have systems in place. They've already worked out the kinks. They have the equipment, the space, the clients, and the employees required to turn a profit. You could even offer the owner to stay on as a consultant for the first year to ensure a smooth transition. And from there, you have the opportunity to bring your fresh perspective, energy, and ideas to help it grow to new heights.

TAKE ACTION

Bonus 1: Grab a free copy of our **Buying a Business Worksheet** to help get you started.

Chapter Three

READY, SET, GO: SIX THINGS YOU CAN START DOING NOW

THINK ABOUT IT:

"Do you want to know who you are? Don't ask. Act! Action will delineate and define you."

- Thomas Jefferson

Quick note: This isn't an overnight process. (We'll talk about that more in a later section.) Get ready to play the long game, and start doing these six things now, so you have the stamina to make it to the fourth quarter.

- **Start mentally preparing.** We discussed this earlier about deciding your WHY, and now it's time to write it out. Be as specific as possible. Read it every day. Have it memorized so you can recall at a moment's notice when you're ready to throw in the towel. Start telling yourself, ***yes you can.***
- **Write out a personal Profit & Loss Statement**. Know exactly what assets you have to work with, what money is coming in, and what expenses are going out.
- **Join a Mastermind Group.** Get support, advice, and encouragement from like-minded professionals.

- **Set measurable goals.** Like hikers scaling Mt. Everest break their ascent into manageable sections, your goals should also be designed to motivate and create accountability. As Tony Robbins says, "setting goals is the first step in turning the invisible into the visible."
- **Spread the word.** It feels safer to play things close to the vest in case you should fail, but social pressure can be a valuable motivational tool. So, share what you're doing. Tell your friends, family, and colleagues. Post it on social media. When people know what you're up to, they'll ask questions, and you'll want to have a good answer for them.
- **Get your house in order.** You're going to be hyper-focused at the beginning, and you need to set expectations for yourself of what you can reasonably commit to during this time. That could mean bringing your family into the loop, so they know you will be busier than normal or hiring someone to make yard work off your plate.

TAKE ACTION

Begin working through this list - just don't attempt to do everything at once. Spending a ½ hour each day over the next 3-4 weeks will add up quickly. Taking giant leaps and diving headfirst might be splashier, but don't underestimate the power of hanging out in the kiddy pool until you're ready.

Chapter Four

MATCHMAKER, MATCHMAKER, MAKE ME A MATCH: WHAT'S YOUR TYPE (OF BUSINESS)?

THINK ABOUT IT:

"The best way to predict the future is to create it."

- Peter Drucker

Everyone has a type. Blonde and leggy. Brawny and brooding. Bald and funny. (Just look at Stanley Tucci.) And while it's important to strike while the iron is hot on all the amazing acquisition opportunities currently available, before you jump into bed with any of them, it would behoove you to first figure out what **type** of business you want to buy.

Starting this process without all the facts will only leave you burnt (and maybe broken-hearted). From the beginning, clarifying what you want - or don't want - in the business you purchase will keep you from making rash decisions in the future.

If you've ever participated in online dating, you have probably been asked to set your preferences. Age. Location. Highest education level. Religion. Kids or no kids. (In a way, you are kind of designing your ideal partner.)

Using this information, the algorithm will hide profiles that don't meet your criteria. Ta-da! You've preemptively weeded out the dates you know have no hope of working out, saving all parties involved the time and energy to focus on the matches that might actually have a shot.

In the same way, designing your ideal business purchase and weeding out those that don't meet your criteria (no matter how pretty it might look on the surface) can save you a lot of time and energy to focus on the ones that are better suited for your needs - and will hopefully make for a long and happy union.

Not sure where to start?

Ask, and ye shall receive. We've got three simple questions to get the 'ol brain juices flowing. Grab a pen and paper (going old-school won't kill ya) and take some time to thoughtfully consider your answers and write them down.

Already have an idea of the type of business you want to buy? Feel free to skip on ahead, but we think it's still a good idea to read and answer the questions. It might confirm what you already know...or, not to be dramatic, **it could save you from making the biggest mistake of your life.** The choice is yours.

Question 1: What Is Your Commitment Level?

Buying a business isn't like buying a pair of pants. You can't simply return it within 7-10 days because you don't like how it looked when you took it home. There is some degree of commitment required. But how much? That is what you need to decide first.

Circle A, B, or C:

A. Full-Time Owner and Operator. This is you if:

- You are transitioning away from your 9-5
- You are approaching this as a new career

- This will be a salary replacement
- You are willing and able to be the operator ***and*** the owner

This is not you if:

- You are limited on time
- You do not know the operation or how to run it without help

B. Part-Time Participant. This is you if:

- You want to commit less time to the day-to-day operations
- You are comfortable hiring others to manage things on your behalf
- You want the ability to be involved in multiple projects
- You aren't interested in leaving your current job completely
- You want access to a second income stream
- You are willing to work with a partner to share some of the responsibilities

This is not you if:

- You don't have a partner you trust
- You don't have an operator to handle day-to-day
- You don't want to split the profits with someone else

C. Hands-Off Investor. This is you if:

- You are seeking passive revenue
- You want to own the business, not necessarily manage it
- Your goal is to invest across multiple companies at once

This is not you if:

- You want complete control over the whole system and operations.
- You think this gets you off the hook from any responsibility. At the end of the day, you are still the ultimate decision-maker.

While the little things may not cross your desk, you can bet the big stuff will. There's no such thing as *truly* passive income.

Knowing this information will help you determine which business opportunities are better suited than others. For example, let's say you can't or aren't ready to leave your job, and you can only be a Part-Time Participant at the moment, and the owner himself currently operates the business you're eying. If you don't have a partner to team up with, or the current profits aren't enough to hire an operator, this would not be the ideal match for you. **It may be a great opportunity - just not a great opportunity for you.**

Question 2: What Is Your Type?

Next, you should focus on the type of business you want to buy. Most will fall into one of these two categories: **Service or Product.**

A **service business** can include - just as the name implies - some type of service: HVAC, car detailing, digital marketing, pet care, plumbing, pest control, lawn care, etc. On the plus side, you don't need to worry about tracking or keeping an inventory, there's a lower cost of entry, and you have more flexibility and customization in terms of pricing your services.

On the other hand, you will likely face more competition since it has cheaper start-up costs. It requires human capital - a.k.a. the person doing the service. And if you can't find or train the right person or people, *that person will be you.* This also means it's harder to scale and grow. You're just one person, after all.

A **product-centered business** offers something tangible to be sold. This can include manufacturing, retail, e-commerce, fabrication, parts, consumables, etc. The benefits of this business model are largely scalability and profitability. As long as you have the materials to make your product, you can continue selling it indefinitely, meaning recurring profit. You can also increase your revenue by creating new products to sell to your current customer base. (Example: Starbucks sells coffee. But they also sell coffee mugs. And travel cups. And gift sets. You get the idea.)

But, as always, there's another side to consider. Inventory means upfront costs to purchase and/or make what you're selling. You also have to deal with shipping and supply-chain issues, trade tariffs if you do business overseas, or ruined products that need to be replaced.

Question 3: What Else Is Important to You?

Other factors to consider include:

Location: Where is your ideal business located? Up the street? In another State? Online?

What Is the Purpose of The Purchase? Do you want to leave your full-time job and replace your income? Or will this be a passive income stream?

Size of Business: What is your ideal revenue target? Remember, the higher the revenue, the more competition you'll have with other eager buyers.

True Profit: What range are you comfortable with? A company may generate $100,000 in revenue every year, but if its operating costs are $65,000, that means its actual profit is $35,000. This might be a good opportunity if you're in a position to be a Hands-Off Investor with little responsibility for the day-to-day, but if you are the Full-Time Owner and Operator, can you get by on a salary of $35,000 a year?

Your Experience: What skills or knowledge do you already have that could add value? How can you leverage your existing expertise to improve the scalability and profitability of a business you acquire?

So, how'd you do? Did you actually write your answers down? Or did you read the questions, think to yourself, *"I'll come back to this later,"* and now you found yourself here, at this paragraph, feeling just a little guilty for skipping such a simple but important part of the process?

Feel free to go back and complete the assignment. We'll be waiting right here.

We cannot stress this enough: These questions might be simple, **but they are important**. They will help you gain clarity and provide some direction on the type of business (or businesses - we're pro-polyamorous) that would be your best match. We want a long and happy union for you, reader. But you gotta put in the work to make it happen.

Remember, this process isn't about just buying yourself a new job. You're doing this to buy a business and, by extension, a lifestyle.

TAKE ACTION

Still didn't do the assignment above? Here's your third reminder to **GET THIS DONE**. Trust us when we say you **NEED** to have a better understanding of the type of business that you're best suited for.

Chapter Five

BEFORE YOU SIGN ON THE DOTTED LINE, ASK YOURSELF THESE 5 QUESTIONS

THINK ABOUT IT:

"We all make choices, but in the end, our choices make us."

- Ken Levine

As we said, the concept of buying a business is simple, but there's still a lot that needs to go on behind the scenes to ensure you're making a wise investment decision.

Don't throw yourself at the first opportunity that presents itself; they're not all home runs. We are trying to work smarter, not harder - and that means doing your research, weighing the pros and cons, and making an intelligent and informed decision.

Like anything in life, a great reward also comes with a significant risk, and there are things you should consider before signing on the dotted line.

1. **Is there cash flow?** If you're buying an asset-heavy business, but they don't have cash coming in, you are essentially starting a business.
2. **What's the competition like?** Can their product or service be easily duplicated? Or have they differentiated themselves enough that there's little risk of copycats?
3. **Do you have any knowledge of the business you're buying?** If not, you might want to consider bringing in a partner who does or finding a solid operator to run the day-to-day.
4. **What is their employment team like?** Will they be open and receptive to changes? Can they be offered a buy-in to stay on? Or will you need to make (and therefore train) new hires?
5. **Is the business a "personal brand?"** If you're purchasing someone's name, and that person has been the sole point of contact, it's likely their customers are relationship-based and do repeat business because of that reason. It will be harder to take over a real estate agency run by one realtor instead of one where multiple realtors operated and did business.

TAKE ACTION

Take out a notebook and jot these five questions down - and then add some of your own. **What would you like to see in the PRO column? What would you consider a CON?** As you begin to entertain and vet deals, refer back to this list to make sure you've covered all your bases.

Chapter Six

TEAMWORK MAKES THE DREAM WORK: WHO TO HAVE (AND NOT HAVE) IN YOUR CORNER

THINK ABOUT IT:

"None of us is as smart as all of us."

- Ken Blanchard

Being an entrepreneur doesn't mean you are doing everything on your own. To be successful, you need to surround yourself with successful people who are aligned with your goals and can help you achieve them. And that means having a strong team of specialized professionals who can help make each investment successful.

Members You Need:

1. Banker
2. Attorney
3. Accountant
4. Advisor (someone who has little to no monetary interest in getting the deal done)

Members You *Could* Need:

1. Operator - hire someone to handle the day-to-day operations if you cannot.
2. Partner - working in tandem with someone else who has different skills can be a tremendous asset and can alleviate some of the workloads.
3. Realtor - can help if real estate is involved.
4. Business Broker - not required, though they sometimes come with the deal. If you have one you've worked with in the past that you trust, you could consider using their services, but it's optional.
5. Insurance Broker - you may want someone in your corner to protect your assets and look out for liability concerns.

Members You DON'T NEED:

1. Investment Bankers - they are not usually involved, but when they are, they're more valuable to the seller, not the buyer.
2. Valuation Expert - remember, you're buying the business for the profit they generate. Even if it is asset-heavy and you're looking to borrow against its worth, the bank will do its own valuation, and theirs is really the only opinion that matters.

When searching for members to join your team, don't just pick the first name that pops up when you search "Attorney" online. Ask around and get referrals. Does your current financial advisor know a good accountant? Who has helped others close similar deals? Stay away from generalists; a jack-of-all-trades is not what we want. Screen thoroughly and treat it like a job interview. Play your "candidates" against each other to create competition to drive up the value they offer or drive down their price. Remember, it's all about surrounding yourself with people who will help you meet your goals.

TAKE ACTION

If you don't already have a trusted Banker, Accountant, Attorney, and Advisor in your corner, start searching for them now. Talk to people in the business. Ask around and request referrals. Read reviews. Network and set up "interviews." Keep a list and take notes. **A good team can make or break you; do your due diligence before bringing them into your operation.**

Chapter Seven

WANTED: BUSINESS FOR SALE, HAVE REFERENCES, WILL TRAVEL

THINK ABOUT IT:

"People who say it cannot be done should not interrupt those who are doing it."

- George Bernard Shaw

As we mentioned previously, approximately 2.5 million businesses are for sale. That can be both an exciting and overwhelming prospect: Exciting because it feels like there are a lot of opportunities to be had. Overwhelming because where does one even begin when dealing with numbers like that?

Hopefully, you followed our advice in section 4 and have already identified the type of businesses you're interested in buying. If you've done that, you can automatically ignore anything that falls outside of that criteria. ***Bada Bing, Bada Boom.*** (See - there's a method to our madness.)

Once you know the TYPE you want to buy, now comes the task of FINDING it. And because it's unlikely it will just fall into your lap (real life isn't an episode of Shark Tank, unfortunately), it will require some time, energy, and patience.

In this section, we're going to lay out a roadmap of sorts to provide some clarity and direction to help prepare you.

Perfect Your Statement of Intent

It's time to craft your elevator pitch. Doing so will:

A) Ensure you yourself know exactly what it is you're looking for, and

B) Will ensure that message is communicated clearly and efficiently.

Take some time to review these questions and write down your answers. (Yes, more homework.) Then practice, practice, practice! You don't want to go into conversations sounding overly rehearsed or robotic, but you also don't want to be flubbing around for answers and give off the impression you have no idea what you're talking about.

- Be specific about what you're looking for: Industry, revenue, location, etc.
- Give them your why: Why are you looking to purchase a business?
- Explain how you can help: Show that you can offer a solution to someone looking to retire or sell.
- Show them proof: What makes you the right person to buy this business?
- Present your *Ask*: What do you want from them?

Not All Sellers Are Created Equal

Know the sellers you want to target. Time is money, and you don't want to waste yours on ones that aren't going to be able to deliver what you're looking for.

An ideal seller will fall into one or more of these categories:

- Ready to retire
- Tired of being in business or burnt out

- Looking for a different opportunity
- Has no successor to take over the business
- More concerned with protecting their legacy/clients/employees than profit

This type of individual will more likely be motivated to sell, and you'll not only get a better deal, but you'll also be providing them a much-wanted out. Win-win.

A less-than-ideal seller will fall into one or more of these categories:

- Highly successful
- Young and energetic
- Still engaged and having fun with what they do
- They do not need to sell

Clearly, this type of individual will be far less motivated to sell their business, so it's probably not the wisest investment of your time and energy to convince them otherwise.

With these criteria in mind, you can stay laser-focused on both the business and seller that will deliver what you want and avoid detouring down a path that leads to a dead-end.

Build Your Network

A strong network is an invaluable resource to help you make connections, trade ideas, meet like-minded people, and promote socialization. And particularly when you're ready to buy a business, tapping into this resource will get your name out there and connect you with those who may be in a position to help.

While the term "networking" may conjure up images of schmoozing with stuffy professionals or awkward conversations over bad wine at Happy Hour mixers, it's really just about forming relationships and opening dialogue. There are plenty of different ways to approach it - and most are completely free!

- Who do you already know? Reach out to family, friends, colleagues, and neighbors. Go through the contact list on your phone or your address book. Send emails, make calls.
- Tap into the power of social media. Facebook, LinkedIn, Twitter. Ask for recommendations, join Facebook groups, share content, and build your following.
- Join Mastermind Groups
- Get plugged into local Chambers of Commerce or Associations.
- Spend time volunteering
- Have conversations with "those in the know": Accountants, bankers, and financial advisors.

There's no right or wrong way to build your network; you can use one or all of these techniques. Some will come more naturally than others, so lean into your strengths and capitalize on those that give you a better ROI.

Explore the Area

In addition to networking efforts, you should also spend time hitting the pavement (literally and figuratively) and be proactive in your search for businesses to buy.

- Utilize sites like ZoomInfo.com or BizBuySell.com to search local and national listings
- Get to know the neighborhood where you're thinking of buying a business. Drive around, walk the streets, and get to know the community. Use Google maps to get familiar with the lay of the land.
- Chat with owners. Just because there isn't a For Sale sign in the window doesn't mean it's off the table.
- Look at your spending habits. What are some of the businesses you love? What places are you already frequenting?

Start making lists. Take note of which opportunities excite you most or if there seem to be any recurring themes.

Dig In!

Now the fun begins. Over time, you should develop a pretty healthy list of viable businesses to consider. Once that happens, you're ready to start digging in for a closer look.

1. Set a goal to look at X number of businesses. You can really make this any number you want but keep it realistic and doable. Somewhere in the 30-40 range is a good place to start.
2. Make a spreadsheet and gather your data. Compiling all the facts and figures into one place will help you comparison-shop between all the different options on the table.
3. Remember to be as specific as possible. Your criteria should whittle that list down to a more manageable number of business owners you'll actually want to spend time in serious conversation with. (In this case, smaller is better!)
4. Once you've narrowed it down to your top 3 or 5 picks, you're ready to start setting up the meetings and take action.

Some Final Thoughts on the Subject

When beginning your search, don't get hung up on doing it perfectly or following these steps line-by-line; it's not a 1-2-3-DONE process. You're going to find that a lot of it will evolve organically over time. Your network will continue to grow; you'll meet new people and be presented with opportunities you wouldn't have considered before, your sphere of influence will expand, and you'll discover new interests. Stay focused but be flexible. You never know where or when your next great deal will present itself.

TAKE ACTION

Bonus 2: Check out our free copy of **50 Places to Find a Deal** to help get you started.

Chapter Eight

STRANGER DANGER: ADVICE ON BUYING A BUSINESS IN AN UNFAMILIAR INDUSTRY

THINK ABOUT IT:

"Without hustle, talent will only carry you so far."

- Gary Vaynerchuk

We're all familiar with the old adage, "*You don't know until you try.*" It's the argument that parents around the world make every evening at dinner to convince their children they'll like those oddly shaped green things on their plates. And it's what we tell ourselves when we're working up the courage to take a risk, like finally ordering The Dirty Shirley (worth it) or sinking a bunch of funds into Voyager (big whoops).

When it comes to buying a business, it's usually recommended you look within the industries you're familiar with. Logically and logistically, this makes perfect sense. You already know the ins and outs of operations, what the markets look like, the challenges, the trends, the competition, and so on. Overall, it tends to be a smoother transition.

But what if you find a really sweet deal on a business you know nothing about? What if you're bored with running a laundromat when what you really want to do is buy a food truck? What if you've hated math ever since the third grade but still ended up as an unhappy accountant who dreams of running a successful e-commerce site?

Listen, there are no rules when it comes to what you can or can't do with your own life. (Mostly, anyway.) And you don't know until you try.

So why not try?

Now that we've hyped you up a bit, let's temper it with some practical guidance. Obviously, acquiring a business is a big, potentially life-changing event and should be treated as such. It's not a decision or agreement you should enter into lightly. So, if you find yourself ready to buy in an industry that's new to you, here are six pieces of advice to keep in mind along the way.

It's OK if You Don't Know the Market

One of the biggest disadvantages of entering a new industry is that you don't know the market. This means you'll be spending a lot more time researching, studying trends, analyzing data, and assessing industry behavior. This can be a time-consuming process, but not impossible. On the plus side, as an industry outsider, you can approach this with fresh eyes and a new perspective because you're not coming into it with preconceived notions of what it "should" look like.

Compare, Compare, Compare

This is a bit of advice we mention ad nauseam, but for good reason. Accurate evaluation is only possible when it's compared to something else. As we mentioned above, having a fresh-eyed perspective is great, but it can be a natural disadvantage because you won't have anything to compare it to. If you're an industry newbie, spend extra time comparing and contrasting with similar businesses. Leaving the world of retail with a 2% profit margin to buy an accounting firm that boasts 8% might look enticing. Until you realize the national average is closer to 18%, so clearly, something's not adding up. (No pun intended.)

Experience is Experience

Don't let the fact that you've not worked in a particular industry dissuade you. While industry-specific experience is obviously a bonus, you shouldn't discount the specific brand of expertise you bring to the table. You may have spent the last ten years in the restaurant business, and now you want to purchase a tire service center. They seem very different on the surface, but apart from better hours and (probably) better margins, there are a lot of similarities. Both require good customer service skills, hiring and firing employees, managing inventory, and working with vendors. Identify your strengths and experience and use that to your advantage.

Don't Be Afraid to Ask for Help

The entrepreneurial spirit is an admirable quality, but it also tends to create the expectation that you must do everything on your own. **Not true.** Investment banker, financier, activist, author of Start-Up Saboteurs and Economic Warfare, and the president and CEO of Blackhawk Partners Inc, Ziad K. Abdelnour said, *"Be strong enough to stand alone, smart enough to know when you need help, and brave enough to ask for it."* Consider getting a mentor or bringing on a co-owner who is an expert in the industry. Work in tandem and combine your fresh outlook with their seasoned experience.

Don't Listen to Everyone

Along the lines of seeking the help of experts, keep in mind you are under no obligation to listen to any of them. **Not all advice is good advice;** even the experts get things wrong now and again. Ultimately, it's your name on the paperwork, billboard, or business cards, and if shit hits the fan, *it's not going to matter that so-and-so advised you to do such-and-such.* You still have to do your own due diligence. Don't take everything at face value, and don't be afraid to ask for competing advice.

Try Before You Buy

If you want some added reassurance that the business you wish to purchase will be a good fit, **give it a trial run.** Inquire if you can observe the day-to-day operations, get a tour, sit in on meetings, or even work alongside the employees. You could even consider taking on some part-time hours in an official capacity to really get a feel for the job.

Entering into a new industry can feel overwhelming and daunting... and exciting, all at the same time. (Life is funny that way.) It will be challenging, but it's not impossible and can open up a whole new world of possibilities for you.

TAKE ACTION

If you find yourself tempted by the siren song of an unbelievably good deal for a business that's outside your usual industry, ***give it a listen before you turn tail and run.*** How can you leverage your experience? Who can you turn to for help and advice? Will you be able to do a "trial run?" Carefully consider this section (and these questions) lest you pass on the career pivot of your dreams.

Chapter Nine

FRANCHISES: TO BUY OR NOT TO BUY? THAT IS THE QUESTION

THINK ABOUT IT:

"When I'm old and dying, I plan to look back on my life and say 'wow, that was an adventure,' not 'wow, I sure felt safe.'"

- Tom Preston-Werner

Buying a business can be a big, life-changing move that will open doors to financial freedom, personal and professional growth, and control over how you spend your time and energy.

It can also be completely overwhelming, especially for first-time owners. Leaving the "safety and security" (*perceived safety and security*) of a 9-5 job and doing a 180 pivot to owning and running the whole show is a lot to take on.

If you have a dream of owning a business but aren't quite ready to take on the whole enchilada, a franchise might just be the way to go. **Think of it as ownership with built-in training wheels: You're still doing the pedaling, but you've got some support keeping you upright.**

Franchising is big business in the United States. An estimated 753,700 franchise establishments employ over 7 million people and output 670 billion dollars. Everything from quick-service food to real estate, convenience stores, and hair salons is up for grabs. But before you make plans to buy a Taco Bell to enjoy unlimited cheesy Gorditas, take a look at our Pros and Cons of buying a franchise and make sure it's the right move for you.

The Pros of Buying a Franchise

No experience? No problem. You don't necessarily need prior business experience to run a franchise. That training is typically provided as they will want to familiarize you with their business model and practices.

Proven to work. When you invest in a franchise, you buy into something that has proven to be successful.

More Support. You'll have the opportunity to tap into a vast network of support from other franchisees.

Advertising and marketing. Your franchisor will likely have an entire team dedicated to handling promotions, creating brand standards, placing ads, etc., making it one less thing you have to worry about.

More accessible financing. In some cases, banks or lenders may be more willing to front money for a franchise as they have an established track record.

Built-in customer base. Hopefully, any business you decide to buy will come with legions of dedicated customers. But a franchise, especially one with wide-reaching name recognition, will give you a much larger pool to play in. (Example: The Mom & Pop diner down the street might be a beloved institution for those in the area, but will out-of-town visitors stop there for a quick bite to eat? Or will they opt for the familiarity of a McDonald's?)

The Cons of Buying a Franchise

You're in control, but also NOT in control. This is probably the most apparent drawback of owning a franchise because, at the end of the day, despite being "the owner," you still answer to someone else. You may not have the freedom to adjust business hours or pricing models, or operating processes as you see fit.

Sharing the profits. You're automatically getting a smaller percentage of the revenue due to royalties that must be paid to the franchisor.

Not enough support. Some franchises will do a better job than others at training, supporting, and equipping you to be successful. Some might make big promises but fail to deliver, leaving you scrambling to figure it out on your own.

Risk your reputation. If another franchise performs poorly or gets lousy press or negative reviews, your establishment will likely get lumped in with them. Consumers will only see the business name, not the individual who is responsible.

Longevity isn't guaranteed. Most franchise agreements have a set number of renewals worked into the contract, but that varies. The decision to renew a franchise agreement is typically up to the franchisor, which means if you're not performing to their standards, they are not obligated to renew it with you.

Like any business transaction of this size, it really comes down to doing your due diligence and research.

- How much can you afford to spend? Remember, you'll need to account for both the startup costs and the franchise fee.
- Is the franchise in a good location?
- Is there room in the market to grow? What is the competition like?
- What type of training and support is offered?

- What is the bottom line? What royalties are going to the franchisor?
- How are other franchisees making out?
- Is the franchise a good fit for your personality or interest level?
- What type of contract is available? How many renewals will be worked into that initial agreement?
- Research the franchise's business model. Does it make sense? Is it something you're willing to go along with?

As the saying goes, there are only two certainties in life, and guaranteed business success is not one of them. Weigh the pros and cons. Seek the advice of others who have walked a similar path. **Research, research, research!** If you do all these things, you stand a much better chance of positioning yourself for success.

TAKE ACTION

Bonus 3: Tune into **Building Wealth and Security Through Franchising with Greg Mohr: Episode 24 of The Liquid Lunch Project Podcast**

Greg, aka, **The Franchise Maven,** has helped 200+ entrepreneurs and corporate holdouts create wealth, financial independence, and security by opening over 450 franchises. In this episode, he explores the ins and outs of franchising, why they are good investments, how to become a successful franchisor, and how to decide if franchising is right for you.

Chapter Ten

WHY BRANDING ISN'T JUST FOR CATTLE

THINK ABOUT IT:

"It takes 20 years to build a reputation and five minutes to ruin it. If you think about that, you'll do things differently."

- Warren Buffett

What do you look for when you decide to make a purchase or hire a company to provide a service? Are you checking them out online, looking at their website, reading reviews, reviewing samples of their work, and learning a little bit more about them and their background?

If you're smart, that's precisely what you're doing. **Because you want to know who or what you're getting into business with.** This is particularly true with large transactions, but even the day-to-day decisions are influenced in this way; how often do you check out a restaurant's Yelp reviews before deciding where to eat dinner? It's a small thing, but the implications are far-reaching.

When going about the task of business acquisition, whether you're just starting out or have been in the game for years, the way you present yourself, **your brand,** and your abilities are critical. Yes, you are the one doing the buying. You are the purchaser. You are the one planning on coughing up a lot of money. But that's just one side of the coin. At the end of the day, you still need to be able to sell yourself. That desire for credibility is a two-way street.

Why is it Important to Build a Personal Brand?

- **It tells people to work specifically with YOU.** Your personal brand is how you'll be represented to the community. It's an opportunity to showcase your talents and expertise, show off your personality, and create a clear picture of the person you are.

- **It helps you stand out from the crowd.** Your personal brand is a way to show what you can do and what you're all about, but it can also show how you're different from the competition and the value you bring.

- **It allows you to understand your own strengths and weaknesses better.** "Knowing yourself is the beginning of all wisdom," according to Aristotle, and he was probably on to something. The process of building your personal brand is a unique opportunity to spend time really getting to know yourself and your strengths, and more importantly, your shortcomings and weaknesses. With this knowledge in hand, you will be more effective in your delivery and will present a more honest and accurate image of yourself and your capabilities.

- **It helps you market yourself more efficiently.** Staying cohesive across all the platforms will make your life infinitely easier, not to mention it looks more professional. Have a set color scheme, font selection, tagline, mission statement, bio, etc. Use it for everything: Your business cards, website, social media posts - any place where you are "advertising" yourself. It might seem like a superficial detail, but when you read the words "Golden Arches" or hear the phrase "Just do it," you know exactly what we're talking about. There's power in recognition.

- **It provides legitimacy and inspires trust.** Having a well-thought-out personal brand puts a face to the name and shows that you're an authority in this area. It shows you're not just another Joe-Schmo off the street or a Snake Oil salesperson trying to swindle a deal.

- **It creates new opportunities.** Building your personal brand, marketing yourself as an authority, showing your successes, and telling your story will lead to open doors and opportunities that can take your business to new heights.

How To Build a Personal Brand

- **Create a website or lead page.** It doesn't need to be anything fancy, but it should be professional and a site where potential customers or sellers can learn more about you.

- **Write a great bio.** Make it catchy, memorable, and succinct.

- **Curate your social media presence.** Facebook, Twitter, LinkedIn, Instagram - whatever you decide to use, make the profile pic, bio, etc., the same across all of them.

- **Share content that has value.** Don't repost just to repost.

- **When you share content that's not your own, always include your own personal spin or anecdote.** Tell your audience why YOU'RE sharing it, what YOUR takeaways were, and why YOU think it's worth reading. Otherwise, you're just promoting someone else as an authority on the subject.

- **Engage with your audience.** Reply to comments. Ask questions. Start a newsletter. Start a podcast. Do live Q&As. Don't let it be a one-way conversation.

- **Build relationships with other brands.** Whether it's another entrepreneur you want to work with or someone you simply admire, building relationships with other experts in the field will help bolster your own legitimacy. Interact with them, share their content, and be intentional like you would in any "real-life" relationship.

- **Provide social proof.** Don't expect people just to take your word for it. You have to earn their trust. This can be achieved via customer testimonials, media mentions, published articles, endorsements, social media shares, or followers.

Some Final Thoughts

If you're someone who is uncomfortable with self-promotion and the idea of "selling yourself" feels, dare we say, a bit braggadocious, **that's even MORE reason for you to heed this advice.**

As we mentioned previously, deals and opportunities aren't going to fall into your lap. You can't sit on your hands and hope for someone to discover you or take you seriously. (You're going to be waiting a very long time.)

Creating a personal brand will provide legitimacy to your business, help you leverage and build partnerships, make you recognizable (online and in-person), and establish you as an expert/authority/go-to person.

This is going to give you more confidence in your abilities.
Which will lead to more deals.
Which will lead to more money.
But above all, it will get you another step closer to the lifestyle you're dreaming of that set you down this path, to begin with.

Tell us again why you don't want or need a personal brand. We'll wait.

TAKE ACTION

Bonus 4: Print out your free copy of our **Building a Personal Brand Workbook** to get the creative juices flowing.

Chapter Eleven

THE ART OF SELLING YOURSELF (LEGALLY, OF COURSE)

THINK ABOUT IT:

"Everything in life is a sale, and everything you want is a commission."

- Grant Cardone.

From sunup to sundown, we are active participants in the world of sales. It doesn't matter what your job title is or how you spend your free time, we are either selling something or being sold something. From Instagram ads to billboards, agreeing to upsize your fast food order, convincing a toddler to eat their vegetables, jockeying for a promotion, deciding which movie to watch, or creating an online dating profile, it all comes down to the art of the sale.

And when it comes to the business of buying a business, it's no different.

If you've followed our advice thus far (hint, you should be), by this point, you will know that the ideal business acquisition often comes down to the ideal seller. (See Round 1, Section 4.) They are someone who is ready to retire, concerned about their legacy, want to protect their employees, or are simply burnt out and ready to move on.

However, unless they are ready to jump ship come hell or high water, even the most motivated of sellers sometimes need a little push or encouragement. This is potentially their life's work, and they may not be willing to hand it over to the first offer that comes along.

Money talks, but it's not the only speaker in the room. For them, it's about more than the price tag.

It's not enough that YOU know you're the right buyer for their business. You need to show THEM why.

How? By building their trust, helping them see your vision, and reassuring them their legacy is in good hands.

To put it simply: ***You have to sell yourself.***

It seems backward, yes. You may be the one with the checkbook, but they are the ones in control.

So, how do you sell yourself without sounding like you're selling yourself?

Before you jump into your first meeting with a potential seller, here are four tips to make it successful - and to keep you from coming across as too desperate.

1. Get Specific About What You Can Offer

To give yourself the best shot at securing the deal, you need to look as attractive as possible; "show off the goods," so to speak. Answer the following questions as it pertains to the business you're looking to buy.

- What skills do I already have? (Copywriting, sales, computer programming, ads, operations, logistics, etc.)
- What is my area (or areas) of expertise? (HVAC, real estate, fashion, tech, finance, etc.)
- What am I passionate about?

- What fills me with purpose?
- Who can I partner with?

This information shows a seller that you've done your research and that you have the experience, skills, partner, or resources to take it on. It gives them confidence in their choice of passing on their life's work to you.

2. Show Them Proof

It's one thing to 'talk the talk'; show them that you've 'walked the walk'. Provide evidence of your success. Talk about your strengths and be specific about the goals you've achieved. "I was able to achieve [insert win here] because I did [X, Y, Z]." The best predictor of future behavior is past behavior. Show them you can back your words up with action.

3. Don't Oversell

Hype yourself up, but be willing to share your failures, too. Show them how you learned from those setbacks and how you corrected the course. And don't be afraid to admit you're not an expert in every single thing. (Nobody likes a know-it-all.) Like Willie Shakespear said, being a "jack of all trades is a master of none, but oftentimes better than a master of one" can actually serve a very valuable purpose. Your unique combination of skills and experience, even if you're not "in the top 1%," may make you ideally suited for their particular business. (Elon Musk can build spaceships, but can he run a floral shop? Our money is on no.)

4. Explain the Benefits of Selling to You

The best business deals are those that benefit both parties. You want to shave some dollars off the asking price. They want to know if their clients will be taken care of or if their employees can keep their jobs. Ask them questions. Find out what their goals are. Know what's important to them, and make sure it's part of your sales pitch. **J. Paul Getty said it best:** *"You must never try to make all the money that's in a deal. Let the other fellow make some money too, because if you have a reputation for always making all the money, you won't have many deals."*

Some Final Advice

"Growth and comfort do not coexist." (Ginni Rometty, former CEO of IBM)

Your first meeting might go very poorly. You may stumble over all your words or accidentally insult the seller or forget every great thing you've done and end up leaving the room feeling like a complete and utter failure who has no idea what they're doing, and maybe you'll just go back to your 9-5 job forever and ever, amen.

Deep breath.

But your second meeting might go better. And your third might go better yet. Like anything in life, the more you do it, the better you get. But you have to be willing to try. You have to be willing to step outside your comfort zone. You have to be willing to sell yourself.

TAKE ACTION

Bonus 5: Listen to **Mastering the Art of Communication with Steve Sims: Episode 34 of The Liquid Lunch Project Podcast:**

Steve is a coach, speaker, podcaster, and author of the best-selling book "Bluefishing: The Art of Making Things Happen." In this episode, he talks about his journey as a "bricklayer from London" to his enormous success as founder of the world's first luxury concierge service -- **and how he's helping business owners achieve their objections through effective communication.**

Chapter Twelve

PROCEED WITH CAUTION: 8 RED FLAGS YOU SHOULD WATCH OUT FOR

THINK ABOUT IT:

"I have not failed. I've just found 10,000 ways that won't work."

- Thomas Edison

Becoming a business owner through acquisition can be a smart move to avoid the hassles and headaches of launching your own startup. With so many new businesses failing within the first five years - not to mention the time it can take even to turn a profit - starting from scratch is risky business, *sans a dancing Tom Cruise.*

That's not to say that acquiring an existing business is a cakewalk; it will come with its own set of unique challenges. But in many instances, the pros outweigh the cons, and buying a business could be your first step to building your empire. (We like to think big here.)

A big part of the purchasing process is doing due diligence. (We do a deep-dive on this a bit later in the book.) Not every opportunity on the market is a good one, and while it might be tempting to jump at the first eye-catching deal that comes along, keep in mind this isn't a new mattress you can try out for 120 days and return for a full refund after four months of fitful sleep. These transactions are a lot of time and (probably) a lot of money, and you want to go into any agreement with a clear understanding of what you're buying.

This is not a time for surprises.

As you're doing your research, you should be mindful of certain red flags. By definition, a red flag is used as a warning of danger. So, if you're at the beach and the red flags come out, don't ask questions, just get your ass out of the water to avoid becoming shark food.

On the other hand, in the world of business, a red flag might mean ***Avoid at All Costs***. But it could also point to an opportunity you can use to your advantage. (Nothing is ever black and white.)

Depending on what you uncover, the red flags that have kept others from sealing the deal could be your ticket to negotiating a better purchase price and working out more agreeable terms that benefit you as the buyer.

Here are eight red flags to keep an eye on.

1. **A needy sales pitch:** A good deal will sell itself. If the owner is laying it on thick and trying too hard, that's a red flag. On the other hand, if they're desperate to sell, why not use that as a bargaining chip to decrease the sales price? If you feel confident you can turn things around, it might be worth the risk if the price is right.
2. **Few repeat clients:** If the business relies heavily on the revenue it makes from one or two customers, that's a potential red flag. The general rule of thumb is that no more than 10% of revenue should come from one customer or 25% from the top five customers. [2]If just one of those were to take their business elsewhere that could significantly affect your bottom line. There

[2] "Customer Concentration." Klipfolio.

may be an opportunity for better marketing and advertising to attract more customers, but you'll have to decide for yourself if it's a risk you're willing to take.

3. **Old or outdated equipment:** If you're buying a business that relies heavily on expensive machinery, the last thing you want to do is fork over funds to update, fix, or replace it. That could be an enormous expense. Ensure you're checking all their equipment thoroughly and inquire about how often they need maintenance or repairs. If it's brand-new equipment, you'll probably pay more but have fewer headaches. If it's older equipment that needs a regular tune-up or is on its last leg, adjust the value of the business and renegotiate the purchase price, or walk away from the deal.
4. **Employee turnover:** What are their average employee turnover rates compared to the industry average? Is it a revolving door of hiring, training, and replacing employees on a regular basis? There is definitely a potential for improvement in this area, especially if it's due to ownership or management issues. But it could also be indicative of a more serious problem and one you need to evaluate if you can correct it.
5. **Community reputation:** Whether it's the local community or the one online, when you acquire a business, you are taking on the good, the bad, and the ugly. And that includes every pissed-off customer they've ever dealt with. When doing due diligence, ensure you're reading reviews and talking to past customers. Does that tire center have a reputation for slow service and rude staff? Do people complain about shipping delays or poor customer service on that e-commerce site? As the new owner, you'll have the opportunity to rebrand and revamp, but you will want to consider whether that uphill battle is worth it.
6. **Declining sales figures:** A business with a solid track record of profitability over a significant amount of time is probably a safe bet. (Albeit, it will come with a higher price tag.) But if you notice those numbers have been in a steady decline, and they've barely been breaking even, that's a red flag. You could chalk this up to incompetent management or poor budgeting. But it could

also signal a larger, systemic problem that you may or may not be able to fix. If it's a challenge you want to take on, you can use their poor sales figures to bring down the asking price.

7. **Contracts and leases:** A lot of businesses will have long-term contracts or leases for properties, buildings, supplies, services, and more. And these relationships will probably come with the deal. You need to know who they're in bed with before you pull back the sheets and hop in (or you might be in for an unpleasant surprise). Do the agreements make sense financially? How much time is left on the contracts? Is there room for negotiation?
8. **Competition and market direction:** This is a double-edged sword. No direct competitors could mean good things…or it could mean that you're buying a Blockbuster and the Movie Gallery on the other side of town has closed up shop. (And we all know how that ended.) Having little to no competition and a majority share of the market is a red flag you should examine closely.

If you encounter any of these red flags while doing your research, don't write them off immediately. While you might initially see them as reasons to run, they can also be opportunities for massive potential. Make sure you're looking at the big picture and carefully consider the pros and cons for yourself, your family, and your goals. At the end of the day, only you can decide if it will be the right choice.

TAKE ACTION

The next time you're researching a deal, **keep an eye out for these red flags.** When one of them pops up, make a pro and con list to help you decide if it's a cut-and-run situation…or if it's safe to dip your toes in the water.

Chapter Thirteen

OOPS, YOU DID IT AGAIN. SEVEN COMMON MISTAKES YOU MIGHT (PROBABLY) MAKE

THINK ABOUT IT:

"Success is walking from failure to failure with no loss of enthusiasm."

- Winston Churchill

Owning a business is a dream for many. And by purchasing one that's already up and running, you avoid the headaches, stress, and risk of starting one from scratch. It's sort of like adopting a teenager instead of a newborn. You already have a pretty good idea of what you're getting into.

But like teenagers, there's an element of the unexpected, and still plenty of *oops* moments. To help you navigate this new territory, here are seven common mistakes to avoid when buying a business.

Mistake #1: Not understanding why the business is for sale.

Seller motivation is always one of the first things you should look into. There are plenty of legit reasons why someone would want to sell their business. They might be planning a cross-country move, want to explore a new industry, or are simply ready to retire. It could also be because it's hemorrhaging money, they're having trouble retaining employees, the production costs are too high, and so on. You might not discover their true motives until you enter the due diligence stage, but from the very start, keep your antenna up and stay alert.

Mistake #2: Not doing due diligence.

Listen, nobody likes doing homework. It was the least fun part of school. But you did it because otherwise, you'd flunk out, be held back a grade, or be grounded from attending the Big High School Dance. Due diligence is like homework for adults. You must, must, *must* (did we mention must) understand the nature of the deal and the nature of the business you want to buy. ***This is not a part to be skipped or rushed.*** Don't take what the seller is telling you at face value. You need to conduct your own investigation into their financials, tax returns, properties, inventory, contracts, etc. It will all become yours when you sign on that dotted line, so you sure as hell want to know what you're getting into. (More on due diligence in Round 2.)

Mistake #3: Not having enough cash flow to operate.

No matter how good of a deal you score, you still need to make sure you have adequate cash to keep the ship afloat. There's always a transition period when buying a business, and you might incur unexpected costs, lose loyal customers, or discover their financials aren't quite what you thought. (Again, this is why you must do due diligence). These can all be a serious blow to your cash flow, so plan to prepare for the unavoidable "growing pains" stage.

Mistake #4: Paying based on forecasted projections.

You should always pay based on the current value of the business, *not the potential of the business.* Some sellers might try to spin you a fairytale of the riches and wonders just waiting to be unlocked in the future - and use that as a bargaining chip to charge an inflated price. If business booms once you take over, it will be because of your time, energy, and hard work. YOU should be the only one who benefits.

Mistake #5: Being desperate for the deal.

You know that phrase, "desperate times call for desperate measures?" Unless a loved one is being held hostage or the alternative is a lifetime of watching Oakland A's games, you should never go into a business purchase out of desperation. You might want this business more than you've wanted anything in your entire life. Still, if that clouds your judgment and prevents you from conducting proper due diligence, securing adequate funding, or crossing all the t's and dotting all the i's, we have a hunch it isn't going to end well. (Maybe watching those A's games isn't the worst thing in the world.)

Mistake #6: Rushing the Process.

There's no one-size-fits-all timeline. It should take as long as it takes. Temper your expectations and give the process the time it deserves to be done properly, otherwise, you're doing yourself a great disservice. As one of our Founding Fathers said, "Great haste makes great waste." (Looking for more specifics? We're covering projected timelines in the next section.)

Mistake #7: Making Too Many Changes Too Fast

In your zealousness and excitement of being The New Guy in Charge, it's tempting to start initiating sweeping changes on Day 1. Ideally, the business you buy is operating on a profit - so clearly, they're doing something right. There will be opportunities for improvement, but you need to approach them diplomatically. Otherwise, you run the risk of alienating and losing good employees and customers.

We hope you don't make these seven mistakes, but remember, **it's all part of the learning process**. It's unlikely you'll close on a deal without any sort of mishap or hiccup. Don't let it discourage you or keep you from pursuing your dream of business ownership. Take the lesson, learn from it, and apply it the next time.

TAKE ACTION

Listen to Brittney Spears, "Oops, I did it again." *(Just kidding.)* As you're exploring business acquisitions, **keep this list handy and regularly check in with yourself** to make sure you're not falling prey to one of these common mistakes.

Chapter Fourteen

GREAT EXPECTATIONS: HOW LONG IS THIS ALL GOING TO TAKE?

THINK ABOUT IT:

"An entrepreneur tends to bite off a little more than he can chew hoping he'll quickly learn how to chew it."

- Roy Ash

Making the decision to buy a business is a big one, especially for first-time buyers. And it's also very exciting - the idea of being your own boss, taking those first steps to entrepreneurship, or generating more income are all appealing goals.

In that excitement, however, it's important to remember that the actual business acquisition process can be pretty lengthy. (This isn't one-click Amazon ordering.) There are a lot of steps to get you to the finish line, including research, market analysis, due diligence, securing funding, and negotiating contracts. Managing your expectations from the starting block will keep you from getting discouraged along the way if it ends up taking longer than you initially imagined it would.

So, give it to me straight. What sort of timeline am I looking at?

There's no one-size-fits-all answer to this question, but on average, you can expect it to take anywhere from 6 - 12 months. That might seem like a long time (and it is), but remember, this is a big undertaking, ***and it should take as long as it needs to.*** Rushing through this process will only end in regret.

Because no two deals are alike, a variety of factors will influence this timeline. Here are four phases of the process that can have the most significant impact on the speed of becoming a business owner.

The Research Phase

Unless you've already pinpointed the business you want to buy, allow yourself 2-3 months in the research phase. You need to consider the industry you're interested in, how you want to operate (for example, brick-and-mortar or e-commerce), geographic location, purchase price, and more. Once you have those criteria established, you'll need to do a scan of the market and start identifying businesses for sale that are a good fit. ***Again, don't rush through this process.*** Take ten or fifteen of your favorites, make a pros and cons list, compare the shit out of them, and then see which ones are left standing.

The Due Diligence Phase

Here's another area you shouldn't rush (do you notice a theme here?). On average, due diligence typically takes 45 - 120 days. Think of this as an extension to the research phase, but on a more granular level. Once you've found the business you're going to purchase, it's now time to collect and analyze information on their finances and operations in preparation for entering into a contract of sale. Remember, if you take over this business, you are inheriting everything, and that could include unhappy employees, vendor debts, and outdated equipment. These factors should be considered when assessing the company's actual value (factors that can be used to your advantage to negotiate a better price, we might add).

Your Motivation

This is sort of obvious, but it is single-handedly the number one influence on the business-buying process. If you're someone who just wants to wait for the perfect deal to fall into their lap, or you're only willing to make half-hearted attempts to locate and analyze potential businesses to buy, there's a good chance you may never see your dreams of ownership come to fruition. Nobody will be holding your hand and dragging you to the finish line; you have to pull up the proverbial boot-straps (or lace up the tennis shoes if we're keeping with the race analogy) and put in the work.

Seller Motivation

Another biggie, as it's one of the factors that's entirely outside of your control. A motivated seller should put forth equal parts energy and effort into closing a deal with the right buyer. If you have a reticent owner who is less than enthusiastic about releasing information about their accounts, operations, etc., it's only going to drag out the process. (And frankly, this probably isn't the type of seller you want to get into business with anyway.)

Final Thoughts

The thought of spending the better part of a year completing the myriad of steps it takes to acquire a business can feel overwhelming - and maybe a bit discouraging. It'll be easy to let the initial excitement burn out, and somewhere along the way, you'll want to throw your hands up in the air and just say, *this is taking too long; screw it.* **Just remember, you don't get prizes for finishing first.** Let it take as long as it takes. Keep your focus on why you're doing it in the first place, and the arbitrary timeline you've built up in your head will begin to matter less and less.

TAKE ACTION

If you already have a timeline in your mind based solely on hopes and dreams and wishful thinking - *chuck it.* **And then reevaluate what it will look like *realistically* based on the information above.**

Extra Shot: How to be a Better Decision Maker

Do your decision-making skills closely resemble a squirrel trying to cross the street? Keep reading.

As a small business owner, you are confronted daily with (what feels like) thousand-and-one decisions -- many of which you don't even realize you're making. But even though you're getting a ton of practice, there is always room for improvement. Effective decision-making is one of the most powerful tools business owners have to drive action; cultivating this skill should not be overlooked.

The process of decision-making falls into two broad categories: Intuitive and Rational. Intuitive decisions rely on a "sixth sense" or "gut feeling." They tend to be more emotional-based and influenced by a person's mood. These types of decision-makers are looking for an outcome that *feels right.* Meanwhile, rational decisions are based on data and facts. It's a more black-and-white approach that has little regard for the emotional consequences and prioritizes an outcome that *makes sense.*

Neither of these processes is inherently better or worse than the other. Each has its place and uses. But the ability to lean into both -- depending on the decision that needs to be made -- is invaluable. Here are a few strategies you can incorporate into your decision-making process to help you become a more effective manager and leader.

Identify the issue.

If you don't know what's broken, you won't know how to fix it. The first and most important step is to clearly identify the problem.

Not all decisions are created equal.

Don't spend valuable time and energy on inconsequential decisions that don't have actual long-term effects. Ever wonder why Mr. Mark Z is always sporting the same sort of look day after day? It's not because he's really behind on laundry; instead, he has removed that decision of what to wear to help keep his mind clear for the more significant, more important decisions. (Clearly, his Metaverse avatar slipped through the cracks.) Think that sounds nuts? Researchers at Cornell University found we make 226.7 decisions each day on just food alone. Always assign a value to the decision that needs to be made; if it's pennies, flip a coin and move on.

Create a deadline

Some decisions will come with their own built-in deadline, but for those that are more open-ended, one of the worst things you can do is not give yourself a due date. By creating a sense of urgency, you'll be more likely to prioritize the issue and give it the time and attention it deserves.

Collect feedback.

While the final outcome ultimately depends on your decision, don't hesitate to reach out and lean on others for advice and feedback. These could be trusted team members, a business coach, advisors, or colleagues who have faced similar situations. Entrepreneurs and small business owners tend to work in silos out of necessity; when you're running a one-man (or one-woman) operation, you learn to depend on you and you alone. And even as you transition to leading and managing a team, it can be easy to fall back on old habits of isolated decision-making. Use whatever resources you have available to assist you with the process -- and that includes using the perspective of others.

Stay neutral -- but only when necessary.

If you're an intuitive-based decision-maker, the ability to stay neutral can be difficult, but it's sometimes necessary to make a wise and pragmatic decision. By removing your opinions and feelings from the equation, you can get a clearer look at the whole picture; you might just be surprised by what you discover. On the flip side, staying neutral could backfire in some cases. Hamilton (the musical, not the Founding Father) said it best: "If you stand for nothing, Burr, what'll you fall for?" Sometimes your opinions, feelings, and beliefs are necessary to make the best right decision. Be discerning about what the situation calls for.

Keep the end in mind.

The ultimate goal of making a decision is to improve an outcome. Dr. Stephen R. Covey's book, The 7 Habits of Highly Effective People, suggests "beginning with the end in mind." In other words, you need to have a clear understanding of your destination. Will this decision get you closer to your goal? Or is it going to leave you stranded at a roadside motel? Even if it pushes you two steps forward and one step back, at least you're still moving in the right direction.

Like so many things in life, there is no one-size-fits-all approach to the process of effective decision-making. And often, we won't know if the decision we reached was the right one until *after* it's been made; it's no wonder that so many of us face decision paralysis (or look like squirrels trying to cross the street). But the worst decision you can make is no decision at all. By incorporating these strategies, you have a better chance of improving your outcomes and making wise, sensible decisions for yourself and your business.

ROUND 2

Buying the Business

Chapter One

IS IT WORTH IT? LET ME WORK IT: HOW TO VALUE A BUSINESS

THINK ABOUT IT

"Don't let others convince you that the idea is good when your gut tells you it's bad."
- Kevin Rose

Understanding the value of the business you want to buy is kind of a no-brainer. You're probably not going to throw down a massive chunk of change without any idea of what profit you can expect to generate in return, right?

(If you are doing that, you should most definitely read this because you need this advice more than most.)

Before we dive in, **the most important thing to keep in mind** is to keep things simple. It can be very easy to overcomplicate and over-analyze every minute detail ad nauseam. This will probably leave you feeling frazzled, overwhelmed, unmotivated, and bowing out before you get to the fun part. **Focus on the pieces that matter most to you.**

The second most important thing to keep in mind is that there is no single right or wrong way to determine the value of a business. Yes, some factors will weigh more heavily than others (profits, for example), but depending on the industry, the market, the seller, and even you as the buyer, there are many things to consider.

Below we've laid out five key areas you should keep in mind to help you determine the value of the business you want to buy.

1. Understand their Competition and Motivation:

- Utilize sites like www.bizbuysell.com to compare other businesses within the same industry, size, revenue, and area.
- How long has their business been on the market? Why hasn't it sold yet? Is the seller not genuinely motivated to let it go? Are they asking too much? Or is it just a business nobody wants to touch with a ten-foot pole?
- This information can be used to help you knock down the amount you offer without sacrificing the value you get in return.

2. Understand their Profit:

- Focus on TRUE profit. This means considering taxes, payroll, expenses, etc.
- The value should be based on current profits, not forecasted projections. It's fun to imagine the "what-ifs," but it shouldn't affect the valuation of the business.

3. Understand their Financials:

- What are their top expenses?
- What assets do they hold? What about liabilities?
- What are their Capital Expenditures? (Funds needed to upgrade or maintain
- What are their profits over the last five years? (Just because last year was a bumper crop doesn't mean its value shouldn't be based on that information alone. We want averages.)

- Do you see any trends, good or bad?
- What does cash flow look like? How much is needed to keep things running?

4. Understand their Debt and Credit Score:

- Check their credit reports through reporting agencies Experian or Equifax. But don't rely on just one; information may vary across the bureaus. We recommend checking out www.nav.com for more information on understanding the scores and their implications.
- What type of debt do they have? Will you be taking on unpaid bills?

5. Understand their Customers:

- Buying a business also means buying its customers.
- What's the ratio of new customers to repeat customers?
- How much do they spend on marketing and advertising each year, and how many new customers does that generate?
- How many customers did they lose? They may have earned 50 new customers over the last year, but if they lost 40, they didn't come out that far ahead.
- Do they rely too heavily on a small handful of customers? If one of those customers were to take their business elsewhere, would it have a significant, negative impact on their sales?
- What are the demographics of their current client base? Are there missed opportunities to market to? Could that be used to your advantage once you take over? (Remember, don't rely too heavily on the what-ifs, but it's definitely something to consider.)
- Have their customer shopping habits changed over time? (More sales online versus in-store, etc.) Do they notice any trends?

Some Final Advice

Read through this list a few times. Start narrowing down to areas you find most applicable and what information matters to YOU as the buyer.

Then make your own list and dive in. Because there's no "one right way" to value a business, it leaves a lot of gray areas. Creating your own valuation system will help you stay pragmatic in your approach, focused on what matters, and aware of the big picture.

TAKE ACTION

Bonus 6: Tune into **How to Determine Your Business's Value with Bharat Kanodia: Episode 55 of The Liquid Lunch Project Podcast**

Bharat is the Founder and Chief Appraiser of Veristrat LLC and has valued over 4,000 companies and assets worth $2.6 trillion - including unique assets like the Atlanta Airport, Uber, *and the Brooklyn Bridge.* In this episode, he teaches our listeners three ways to value any company or asset and why building trust is a critical part of the process.

Chapter Two

HOW TO DIY AN LOI: WRITING A LETTER OF INTENT

THINK ABOUT IT:

"It's more effective to do something valuable than to hope a logo or name will say it for you."

- Jason Cohen

When you're ready to move forward with acquiring a business, constructing a Letter of Intent (LOI) is an essential piece of the process. It's an "informally formal" way to specify your intentions and lay the groundwork for upcoming negotiations and purchases.

What is an LOI?

A Letter of Intent is simply an "agreement to agree." It's a document that outlines and identifies the terms of an agreement between two or more parties and can help minimize future misunderstandings and streamline the final deal.

Think of writing an LOI as courting. Someone special has caught your eye, you've spent some time chatting them up and getting to know them (aka, research), and there seems to be mutual interest between both of you. You like what they're selling. They like what you're offering. And both parties have agreed to dinner, drinks, or a picnic on the beach. You go into the date with the hope of something permanent, like marriage (aka, taking ownership of the Business), but nothing is legal, official, or permanent at this stage.

What Goes in an LOI?

While the specifics of each Letter of Intent will vary based on the type of business you want to buy, here is a general guideline of items you may want to consider including.

Introduction:

You should begin your LOI with a brief introduction that outlines the purpose of the document, clearly identifies both Buyer and Seller, identifies the Business, and explains what the LOI will cover.

Timeline:

Establish a reasonable timeline for negotiations and the transaction to be completed. This could include dates for specific goals or benchmarks that must be reached and/or a final target deadline. You may also want to allow for extensions of these deadlines if it becomes necessary.

Purchase Price:

Obviously, this is a biggie and one you should pay very close attention to; it's a lot more than just slapping a number on the letter and moving on. How is it being paid? When is it being paid? All in cash? Seller financing? Will it be contingent on the Buyer getting funding? Will it be issued in installments? What happens if due diligence (covered later) uncovers information that impacts the value of the company and therefore impacts what you are willing to pay? Be specific.

Due Diligence:

Doing due diligence is where you really dig deep and get to know the Business from the inside out. (Throwing it back to the courting analogy, it's getting past the polite small talk about the weather and confessing to your deepest, darkest secrets.) You'll be going over their financials and records with a fine-tooth comb to ensure you have a complete understanding of the Business you intend to acquire.

Within the LOI, you should specify what the due diligence process will include and that you'll have the Seller's full cooperation to provide the required documentation. (See the next section for a Due Diligence Deep Dive.

Confidentiality:

Both parties may wish (and should!) to agree not to disclose the proposed business acquisition to the general public. It should also be noted that all information collected will be kept confidential and used for the intended purpose - and that confidentiality will remain in place even if the deal isn't finalized.

Exclusivity, Contingencies, and Termination:

During the due diligence process, the LOI should acknowledge that the Seller cannot enter into negotiations with any other Buyer (it's time to make your relationship exclusive!). It should also specify that there is no obligation to finalize the agreement if the Buyer is dissatisfied with any of the findings and that both parties have a right to terminate and walk away.

Simple examples of Letters of Intent are plentiful on the World Wide Web, and free and fee-based templates are available for download if you don't want to start yours from scratch. Depending on the deal's complexity, it may be worth having it drafted by a professional, or, if you're a first-timer, by someone who has written one before. Remember, the LOI is not a legally binding agreement you're signing; rather, it's meant to lay the groundwork so a long union can be reached and both parties can live happily ever after.

TAKE ACTION

Bonus 7: We did the heavy lifting for you! Feel free to use the copy of our editable **Letter of Intent Template** found with the other bonus materials.

Chapter Three

WE ARE NOW ENTERING NEGOTIATION STATION

THINK ABOUT IT:

"You do not get what you want. You get what you negotiate."

- Harvey Mackay

By this point, you've gone through the process of determining the type of business you want to buy, where to find them, and how to assess their value. Equipped with this information in hand, you're now ready to go into the fun part: **Negotiation.**

Ok, depending on your personality, this might not actually be the fun part. Still, it's definitely not the part you can avoid, especially if you want to reach an advantageous deal. (Which, of course, you do.)

One thing to remember before we dive in is that negotiation is not an exact science. There isn't a checklist you can follow that will guarantee a positive outcome every single time; there are far too many variables at play. So, with that in mind, dismiss the notion that there's only "one right way" to do this.

There isn't.

A quick Google search will give you more advice than you want to know about successfully negotiating a deal: Don't speak first. Words you should never say. Know when to talk away. Do your homework and come prepared. The list goes on.

But because we believe in keeping things simple, **we narrowed it down to four key areas we feel are essential** to help you negotiate the deal of your dreams.

1. Understand the Seller

Negotiating a successful deal is about more than throwing out impressive offers. Money is important, yes - but there are likely other "unrealized" reasons a seller wants to sell. *It's your job to figure out what those reasons are, and you can use them as part of the negotiation.*

- **Why are they selling?** Financial reasons? Retirement? Health issues? New opportunities? Are they simply burnt out?
- **What will their life look like post-sale?** Less stress? More time for family? Freedom to pursue other interests?
- **What do they want from the buyer?** Keep their employees employed? Stay on in a part-time capacity? Leave their name on the building?

As an aside, please do not enter your meeting with a clipboard and a list of these questions to run down like you're conducting an interrogation. Work them in naturally. Keep things conversational. They'll feel more comfortable opening up, and you can discover the actual reasons behind their desire to sell.

2. Highlight the Give, Remember the Get

The most successful deals are ones where both parties walk away satisfied. As you get to understand the seller and what they genuinely want and need, you have an opportunity to fulfill that for them. **Remind them of what they gain by selling YOU their business**. For example:

If they mentioned they wished they had weekends free to watch their grandkids play baseball, remind them this deal gives them back their time.

If they are burnt out, remind them they have the opportunity to walk away and improve their mental health.

If they want to ensure their legacy continues and their customers are taken care of, show them how you are ready to make sure both of those things happen.

These are elements of the deal you can't put a price tag on. And as the buyer, you can use this information to help knock down the final sale price to an amount that makes it a wise investment for you - while also giving the seller what they really want. Win-win.

3. Focus on Price OR Terms

Sometimes, the best advice is the simplest:

Negotiate for the price you want and be willing to sacrifice some of the terms.

OR

Negotiate the terms you want and be willing to pay more to close the deal.

4. Don't Fall in Love at First Sight

It might be fine for a Disney movie, but **"love at first sight" has no place in negotiations.** It's important to stay pragmatic - you're not doing yourself any favors by making a doe-eyed deal. We can really only tell if something is "good" or "bad" by comparison, so before you sign the dotted line with hearts over the i's, make sure you compare it to similar deals. Don't let your desire for the business get in the way of making sound, logical decisions.

Last Thoughts

Again, there is no right way or wrong way to about it. At the end of the day, the best way to get better at negotiation…is to negotiate.

TAKE ACTION

If you're not at the negotiation phase yet, just remember to circle back and re-read this section as you begin to prepare. **Do research. Make notes.** And have a genuine desire for both parties to walk away satisfied. You'll be well on your way to successfully negotiating and closing your first deal.

Chapter Four

DOING A DUE DILIGENCE DEEP DIVE

THINK ABOUT IT:

"Formal education will make you a living; self-education will make you a fortune."

- Jim Rohn

If you're someone who hated homework in high school - we've got some bad news for you.

The expression "what you don't know can't hurt you" might be valid for a lot of things, but when it comes to buying a business, what you don't know is precisely what could bite you in the ass.

Performing due diligence is one of the most critical steps when purchasing a business. I don't care if the dude you're buying from is your brother's best friend's sister's step-uncle, who you've known since you were in diapers. You should always, ALWAYS do your homework before making anything official. A misrepresentation of facts or figures - intentional or otherwise - is always a possibility. Protect yourself from agreeing to a crap deal. Remember, it's not personal - it's business.

When is it done?

Due diligence is typically one of the final phases of your business acquisition journey. You've already scoped out what you want to buy, spoken with the owner, made an offer, and negotiated the price and terms. All of that, however, is contingent upon said owner providing you with accurate facts and figures about the overall health of the business he's selling you. **Enter Due Diligence.**

Why is it so important?

When you're buying a company, you assume ownership of everything. EVERYTHING. That might include profits, valuable contracts, and inventory. (Yay!) That might also include back taxes, outdated equipment, and terrible profit margins. (Not yay.)

You should never take anything at face value, which is why you must perform your due diligence to confirm that what you're paying for is what you're getting. You may discover they're in better shape than you thought. Or you might find it's a sinking ship, and you didn't pack any life vests.

When conducting due diligence, you want to focus on three main areas: Finances, Operations, and Legal.

1. Finances

Review Profit and Loss Statements: Review revenue, gains, expenses, and losses and compare quarter by quarter over the last five years. Do you notice any trends? Their numbers might be "good" right now, but has there been a steady decline over the last year that indicates a problem of things to come? Are their expenses increasing? Are profit margins holding steady? Or are there noticeable (and unexplained) dips?

Review their Cash Flow: Positive cash flow means the business has more money coming in than going out. Negative cash flow means the company is spending more than what they're bringing in. While it's unlikely that you'll acquire the actual cash when you buy the business, it should still be reviewed and analyzed to understand better what you can expect once ownership transfers over. Depending on your own financial situation, you might need to rely on a certain amount of cash flow in the early days. Make sure there will be enough.

Review Balance Sheets: This is where all the business's assets, liabilities, and equity will be listed. Assets bring value to the company (inventory, equipment, trademarks, patents, etc.). Liabilities are what the business owes (unpaid invoices, loans, etc.). And equity is simply the difference between the two.

Review Taxes: It's not fun (unless you're in the accounting sector), but it's not something you should skip over. While the IRS loves making sure they get every cent they're owed, people still manage to cheat (or disregard) the system, and any back taxes or tax liens the business has will become your problem. (And believe us, the IRS will figure it out eventually). You'll want to ensure all tax payments are current and review payroll, property, and employment taxes for any discrepancies.

2. Operations

Time to see how the sausage gets made. This is an opportunity to deep-dive into the operation's inner workings. Depending on the type of business you're buying, you may want to review the following:

- **Supply Chains & Logistics** (Are they experiencing any disturbances that are impeding their ability to operate and deliver?)
- **SOPs** (Do they have Standard Operating Procedures that not only make sense but are being followed?)
- **Equipment** (The laundromat you want to buy may have 45 machines, but are half of them on their last legs and will need replacing soon?)
- **The Site** (Is the space conducive to current operations, or is it too small/too large? Does it need upgrades or repairs?)

- **Their Employees** (Are they happy and satisfied with their work? Are there tenured employees who will be an asset to you? Or will you need to let them go and start hiring from scratch?)
- **Their Customers** (Check out online reviews. Do they have a lot of repeat customers? How often do they acquire new business? Do they rely too heavily on just a few customers? What would happen to their bottom line if those customers took their business elsewhere?)

3. Legal

Surprises are only fun when they're good surprises, and the last thing you want to do is uncover a shitty lease agreement or contract three months into being the new owner. If you haven't already, you may want to involve an attorney in this process, as it can get pretty technical and cumbersome. You should be looking at the following:

- The aforementioned lease agreements
- Contracts with vendors, suppliers, etc.
- Stockholder agreements
- Company by-laws
- Patents
- Licensing or franchise agreements
- Any past or pending litigation against the company or initiated by the company.

You should expect to spend anywhere from 45 - 180 days on due diligence. Perhaps less if it's a smaller deal - or up to six months if you're taking on a large or complex business. Either way, it's important not to rush the process. ***Be efficient, but don't get sloppy.***

Again, it might be your brother's best friend's sister's step-uncle who you're buying from, but you should never just "take their word for it." What you uncover during due diligence can not only give you room to renegotiate terms and costs with the seller - it can also keep you from making a huge mistake. Don't go into it blindly. Put in the time, do the homework, and make the best deal possible.

TAKE ACTION

Bonus 8: Print out a copy of the **Due Diligence Checklist** to keep yourself on track

Chapter Five

SHOW ME THE MONEY! A TRADITIONAL APPROACH TO FUNDING THE DEAL

THINK ABOUT IT:

"There's always a way - if you're committed."

- Tony Robbins

Moment of truth time. You did the research. You put in the work. You compared and contrasted the businesses until your eyes went crossed. Negotiations are finished, and both you and the seller are ready to make it official.

It's time to talk about financing.

The money has to come from somewhere, and since no one has figured out how to grow it on trees (yet), we need alternative methods to fund our business buys.

There is a surprisingly long list of ways to secure funding to purchase a business - and none of them are "more right" than others. (Though, if we're being honest, some of them are complete garbage, so we don't talk about those.) Ultimately, the route you decide to take will depend on factors like the type of business, the amount you need to borrow, credit history, collateral, etc.

Here are the Top Four traditional methods we recommend exploring as a starting point.

SBA 7(a) Loans:

Small Business Association Loans are an obvious choice. (It's literally in the name.) These programs are designed specifically to make it easier for small businesses to get the funding they need.

Here's how it works: The lender makes the loan, and the SBA guarantees it will repay up to a certain percentage if you default on that loan. (85% for amounts up to $150,000 and 75% for amounts greater than $150,000.) But this isn't a get-out-of-jail-free card. They will do anything to collect your debt, only falling onto the guarantee if all options have been exhausted. It's still a loan. It still needs to be paid back. And it still needs to be used responsibly. You can borrow up to $5 million, and the approval turnaround time is typically 5-10 business days.

There are many different places to access SBA loans, and you should rarely (if ever) go through a bank that doesn't do a lot of them. We suggest visiting www.SBA.gov for the 100 most active SBA 7(a) lenders in the United States. It's updated quarterly and shows you those who know what they're doing - and, more importantly, those who don't.

Under the umbrella of the SBA loans, there are two more worth mentioning:

- SBA Express: The express option is worth considering if you need immediate financing and can't wait around for the 5-10 day approval from the traditional 7(a) loan. Turnaround time is typically 36 hours, and you can get a max guarantee of 50%.
- Veterans Advantage: If the business is a least 51% owned by active military, veterans, reservists, etc., you can secure an SBA loan with reduced feeds.

With the guarantee of an SBA loan, there are some strings attached. (Aren't there always where the government's concerned?) To qualify for a 7(a) loan, you have to meet specific eligibility requirements, including:

- Operate for profit
- Be a small business, as defined by SBA
- Do business in the United States
- Have reasonable invested equity
- Be able to demonstrate a need for the loan proceeds
- Use the funds for a sound business purpose

Traditional Commercial Loans

Back in the day (we're dating ourselves), the only way to get your hands on a large amount of cash was to either rob the bank or borrow from the bank. And since we don't condone theft, we'll focus on the latter of the two.

Bank loans are the OG of money lending and can still be a great option. You don't have the same eligibility requirements as you would with an SBA loan, so you have more freedom to use the money at your discretion. You can also improve your credit score by making on-time payments.

But there are some downsides compared to SBA loans (and remember, the only way we can tell if something is "good" is by comparison). Because they don't come with a government guarantee, it may be harder to get approval from the lender. A good credit score, collateral, and strong financials may be needed to secure the amount you want to borrow at a reasonable interest rate.

Peer-to-Peer Lending

One of the newer options on the table, peer-to-peer lending, has really changed how we borrow money over the last several years. Rather than relying on a banker in a business suite to crunch the numbers (and potentially crush our dreams), we can tap into the power of the people - and the power of their pocketbooks.

Between 2006 and 2018, lending platforms provided more than $48 billion in consumer loans, and it's expected to increase to $150 billion per year by 2025[3]. P2P lending is excellent for investors who are looking for ways to make their money work for them - and great for borrowers who may have a more challenging time obtaining financing via a more traditional route. They can also offer lower interest rates and origination fees due to competition between lenders.

Go to www.moneyunder30.com for an overview of eight of the best peer-to-peer lending sites. You can compare APRs, term amounts, how much you can borrow, and which one is best for you and your particular needs.

Seller Financing

This last option is a bit more unconventional than the previous three but has plenty of advantages going for it. Rather than going to a bank, lender, or another entity to put cash money in your hand to buy a business, you will work directly with the seller to "pay them off" over time.

After you take ownership of the company, you'll enter into an agreement that uses your future profits to pay the seller, with interest, over a set amount of time (possibly monthly or quarterly payments over X number of years). No credit checks. No lengthy approval processes. Less red tape overall and more motivation for the seller because the interest you pay is going into their pockets, not the banks.

There are some downsides. Seller financing typically requires a substantial down payment, so if you don't have that type of money sitting in the bank, you'll need to find it another way. Additionally, businesses sold via seller financing will probably come with a higher price tag since they save the buyer the hassle of obtaining financing.

---

3 "Best Peer-to-Peer Lending of December 2022." U.S. News.

These four traditional funding options are just the tip of the financing iceberg. If you really want to get creative (and pay nothing upfront), continue to the next section.

TAKE ACTION

Bonus 9: We've put together a list of **16 Funding Solutions from Shield Advisory Group** with terms and details to help get you started on your path to secure financing.

Chapter Six

HACKING & STACKING THE SYSTEM: A LESS TRADITIONAL (BUT MORE FUN) APPROACH TO FUNDING

THINK ABOUT IT:

"In the end, a vision without the ability to execute it is probably a hallucination."

-Steve Case

What if we told you that you could buy a business and use ZERO dollars of your own money?

Before you ask - yes, it's completely legal. (Or, at least, the way we do it is.) It just requires a bit of outside-the-box thinking (a Liquid Lunch Project favorite!) and some creativity.

We like to call this process "Hacking and Stacking." We're hacking the traditional system and using stacking methods to finance our acquisitions without paying out of pocket.

What does this look like?

Think of it as you would when stacking a sub. (Or hoagie, for our Philly-area friends.) The more layers you give it, the more delicious it becomes. Bread and cheese and meats and pickles and peppers and, well - you get the idea. Each component brings something to the table to create mouthwatering goodness. In the same way, you can "stack" multiple approaches and angles to get the financing you need, and the price point you want.

Let's say you want to buy a business through seller financing, but they want a 40K deposit to make the deal happen.

Do you plunk that amount down on a credit card? (I mean, you could, but probably not wise.)

Instead, you could take out an SBA 7(a) loan for the total amount. You'll have enough to cover the 40K deposit and can continue paying the seller over the agreed-upon number of years using the profits from the business. And since the SBA loan money is just sitting with you in your bank, you have some breathing room to cover unexpected costs or even reinvest in the business itself. ***Hack and Stack, baby.***

Here are twelve less-traditional financing options you can use to hack and stack your own deal.

1. **The Equity Earn-In Approach**

This method is relatively straightforward. You agree to contribute a specified amount of effort, time, or resources into the company in exchange for a certain percentage of equity. This can be measured in several different ways.

- Time-Based: You need to satisfy the agreement to work X number of months/quarters/years to receive equity in the business.
- Milestones: These could be personal milestones (you complete certain events or projects) or company-wide (milestones were met for the entire company).

- Revenue or Profit: You receive equity once you help the business attain a revenue goal or generate enough profit.
- Immediate Equity: Depending on the business and the deal, you can negotiate immediate equity in the company if what you're offering is valuable enough!

2. **The Lease Approach**

Much like leasing a car, you agree to make a number of payments over a certain amount of time. This is an excellent option for buyers who may not want to, or be able to, commit to the full purchase price out the gate while also allowing them to experience what it's like to run the business without taking ownership (yet).

When the agreed-upon terms have been met, you can either opt to buy in at the prearranged price, negotiate to extend the lease, or relinquish control of the business to the owner. Not all sellers will go for the lease option, especially if they are anxious to sell the business and don't want to run the risk of you opting NOT to buy it in the end. Still, others may welcome the opportunity for regular monthly income on a business they still technically own but aren't responsible for running. This is another example of why it's crucial to know the seller and their goals so you can use it to negotiate a deal that's a win-win for both parties.

3. **The Asset Negotiation Approach**

Does the business you're buying have a lot of assets you do not need? Use that to your advantage! You can:

- Remove them from the equation to decrease the price you pay to the seller. (Just make sure you are valuing them at *actual* cost. Remember, the higher the value of the assets, the more you can deduct from the final amount.)
- Offer to sell the assets on behalf of the seller. You'll give them the proceeds while retaining a certain percentage of the sale, sort of like a "finder's fee" for being the middle-man in the

negotiation. This appeals to sellers who don't want the hassle of selling off the assets themselves.

4. **The Supply Approach**

This approach needs a bit more legwork to pull off but can significantly impact the final purchase price if you play your cards right. It's all about bringing something to the table that only you can. This can show up in a few ways:

- Are you helping a business grow that's not yours? Are you sending referrals and customers their way without enjoying any of the revenue? If it's a significant amount, they may very well be open to a conversation about exchanging your contributions for equity in the company. *(Especially if it's casually dropped in conversation that you could start sending those customers elsewhere.)*
- Provide a product or service for the company's customers and offer to split the revenue. This is great for both buyers and sellers. As the buyer, it allows you to test the demand for the product or service. For the seller, they're raking in 50% of the profits with none of the effort. (Who wouldn't love that?) If it turns out to be a massive success for both parties, use it to negotiate a buy-in with the company.
- If you don't have a product or service of your own to offer but have identified a 3rd-party vendor you think would be beneficial to the company, offer to negotiate an agreement between the two, with them splitting profits and you taking a finder's fee. That finder's fee can be arranged with both the company AND the 3rd-party. (No shame in double-dipping!) It's another win-win because they both see increased profits while doing none of the work. And you can use your share as a down payment to acquire the company.

5. **The People Approach**

If you'll need to hire someone to operate the business or know of someone interested in becoming a business owner themselves, offer them immediate equity in exchange for their investment of capital. This works especially well for existing employees who know the business inside and out and may jump at the chance for a stake in the company. This will decrease the price you need to pay out-of-pocket, and you'll hopefully end up with a great operator or partner.

6. **The Convertible Debt Approach**

Before you get too excited, let us clarify we are not telling you to take out a loan for a brand-new sports car. (What we're talking about is far less sexy, I'm afraid.) Convertible debt means that you borrow money from a lender with the intent that you'll repay all or part of the loan by "converting it into a certain number of its common shares at some point in the future." If your business is projected to see an increase in its stock's values, this could be a very enticing transaction for lenders.

7. **The Rent Deferral Approach**

This only works if you purchase a business requiring a brick-and-mortar presence. (Think storefront, warehouse, factory, etc.) It's well worth your time and energy to approach the property owner and request a postponement of rent for a set period of time in exchange for a lease extension or renewal. As the business's new owner, you'll likely want to explore other leasing options - and the landlord knows that. Use it to your advantage.

8. **The Sublease Space Approach**

Another one that only works if you have a physical property. If the new business you're acquiring has more space than you need, consider leasing out a portion of it to a third party. That's steady revenue you can pump right back into your rent, purchase price, etc.

9. **The Royalty Financing Approach**

Traditionally, investors lend money in exchange for an equity stake in the business. But with royalty financing, they'll instead receive a percentage of the business's revenue. This is an excellent option if you aren't too keen on giving up any portion of ownership of the company.

10. **The Third-Party Guarantee Approach**

If you have a loan with the seller, but they want some sort of guarantee that you are unwilling or unable to provide, approach a third party to step in. In exchange for interest, equity, or something else of value from you, the third party will pledge to guarantee that the loan will be repaid if you cannot. Sometimes it's good to have a third wheel along for the ride. (And sometimes it's good to BE the third wheel. Being a third-party guarantor for another business can be a lucrative arrangement.)

11. **The Fractional Rights Approach**

Just as investors can now own a slice of a big-name stock (rather than the whole shebang), that same principle can be used to sell "rights" to your company. Obviously, you don't want to hand over the entire pie, but if someone is interested in a specific fraction of your business (like your email list, for example), you can sell them the rights to it for an agreed-upon amount of time and price.

12. **The Angel Investors Approach**

These are typically successful individuals with high net worth who are willing to invest their money into a company in exchange for ownership shares. It's a similar process as venture capitalists, except they use their OWN money (venture capitalists risk other persons' money), and the amount they invest is typically lower. Just be mindful of how much equity you're willing to give up in exchange for the cash.

One More Time for the People in the Back

We said it before, and we'll say it again (and again): Compare, compare, compare. Funding isn't one-size-fits-all. This is a HUGE investment you're undertaking and rushing the process or being sloppy is going to bite you in the ass.

Take a close look at all of your options on the table. Get creative by stacking and combining financing options. Try a few on before tearing off the tags. Consider prepayment penalties, interest rates and terms, and all the nitty-gritty details before signing any dotted lines or entering into any formal agreement. You'll thank us (and yourself) later!

TAKE ACTION

Grab a piece of paper (*we love giving you homework*) and **start making a list of the funding options you want to explore**. Check terms, credit requirements, details, etc., and then get creative! Start brainstorming ways you can stack two or more to create your perfect funding solution.

Extra Shot: Valuing Your Customers

We've all heard the phrases, "The customer is always right," or "Customer is King," - and there's a simple reason for that: Businesses don't survive if they don't have customers. And because most business owners want to survive, they'll (usually) do what needs to be done to keep their customers.

Of course, we know the customer isn't ALWAYS right, but now's not the time to split hairs. At the end of the day, if you want to keep your doors open and the till humming, you need to keep them happy. That doesn't mean you must acquiesce to every ridiculous demand or unjustified complaint, but as a whole, learning how to value your customers is a critical component to long-term success.

Whether you've just acquired or started a new business or have owned one for years, it's never too late to put the following five suggestions into practice.

Understand Your Customer: This is Marketing 101, but an important step that should not be skipped. Understand who you're selling to. Create your ideal client profile. Start with broad strokes, then get more specific. What are their demographics? What are their spending habits? How do they shop, online or in-store? The more you know about them, the more you can predict what they want or need.

Ask for Customer Feedback: It's pretty simple. Find out what you're doing right - *then do more of that.* Find out what you're doing wrong - *then do less of that.* Collecting customer feedback is one of the most valuable resources a business owner can access. Don't wait around for the public reviews. An unhappy customer is 2-3 times more likely to leave a review than a happy customer. And when you consider that around 95% of consumers read those reviews five before making any purchasing decisions, that can be very detrimental to your business. Be proactive and course-correct when needed.

Improve the Customer Experience: Unless you have a very specific niche or a complete monopoly on the market, you probably have competition. And if it's easier or more convenient for them to do business with options B or C, that's probably what they're going to do. You need to analyze your systems and processes. Are you set up to collect multiple types of payments? Is your website optimized for a mobile experience? How easy is it to reach customer service? How easy is it to make a return? Are your business hours conducive to your customer's shopping hours? (These are examples of invaluable feedback you can collect from your customers!) Think about how you can improve their overall experience, so the transaction isn't a chore, *and* they look forward to doing business with you.

Reward Loyal Customers: *"Make new friends but keep the old. One is silver, the other is gold."* Repeat customers are more valuable to your business. Case closed. Yes, you want to continue attracting new customers, but do not sink all your marketing dollars into that category. Not only is it five times more costly [4]to get someone new through your doors, but

[4] Landis, Taylor. "Customer Retention Marketing vs. Customer Acquisition Marketing." Outbound Engine. April 12, 2022.

the success rate of making the sale is only between 5-20%. (As opposed to 60-70% to an existing customer.) Focus on retention and thanking your loyal customers with thoughtful rewards they'll actually appreciate. This could include access to early savings, invites to VIP events, referral bonus programs, or a special level of service. Remember, they could go anywhere, but they chose you. Thank them.

Educate Your Customers: The sales receipt might be final, but that doesn't mean the transaction has to end. You want to make sure your customer understands the full value of the products or services they purchased from you. This will increase their overall satisfaction - *which is always good for business.* It could be as simple as explaining the details in person when they're checking out, or an automated email delivered to their inbox with additional information about features and benefits. This goes for new products and services, too. Don't just market to your customers - educate them. Explain how YOUR company has what they require to solve a problem or meet a need. Empower them to make the right decision. If you do it right, they'll choose you every time.

Valuing your customers isn't necessarily catering to their every whim. (That's exhausting and, frankly, a poor business decision.) Rather, it's being intentional about understanding their needs and providing a solution they can feel good about.

ROUND 3

Growing the Business

Chapter One

SO YOU BOUGHT A BUSINESS. NOW WHAT?

THINK ABOUT IT:

"It's not about ideas. It's about making ideas happen."

- Scott Belsky

Congratulations! You bought it. It's yours. The paperwork has been signed, the deal has been done, the arrangements have been made, and you are now the shiny new owner of [insert business here.] You just put in a helluva lot of time, sweat, and energy into making this happen, so take a moment to lift a glass of something bubbly in honor of yourself. *Salute! Santé! Prost! Sláinte! Salud! Skål!*

So now what.

Now we turn our focus to some of the nitty-gritty details. Not to add any pressure to the situation, **but the first 90 days are critical to setting the foundation for your long-term success.** As you begin to settle into your new role as owner, your top priorities over the next three months may include:

- Getting to know the Team.
- Hiring an operator and/or preparing to take over those tasks yourself.

- Evaluating (and improving) systems and processes.
- Taking a deep dive into the daily finances.

It's OK to take your time with it. If you've done your due diligence, the business is already profitable as-is, and you can afford to spend these first weeks getting to know it from an insider's perspective.

Here are five areas we believe you should focus on in the early days of the acquisition.

Should You Hire an Operator?

Actually, the *real* question is, do you have enough room in your budget to hire an operator? This is (hopefully) something you already considered during the exhaustive research phases of the acquisition, but it bears repeating. Once you account for all expenses and costs, is there enough left over in the budget to hire an operator that can run the day-to-day? (If you weren't prepared to handle operations yourself, we hope the answer is a resounding yes.)

If this is already something you've accounted for, here's a gold star and a few tips to help you find and hire one.

- **Where to look:** This answer could fill a whole chapter, but here's the skinny. Start with people you know and trust. Network and ask around. Find people in similar roles who may be looking for a new opportunity. Use sites like CareerBuilder or Indeed to place your ads and search resumes. Advertise on social media.
- **What to look for:** Experience vs. Potential. Which option you choose will depend on your budget and how much time you have to invest in the process. An experienced candidate will come with a bigger salary requirement but will probably require less attention and hand-holding from you. A candidate with potential will come with a smaller "price tag" but would likely need training and more support in the beginning.
- **Know what questions to ask:** Get a good picture in your mind of your ideal candidate, then formulate your own list of interview

questions based on what's most important to you. Do they have proven leadership experience? What are their long-term goals, and do those align with the company? How do they troubleshoot problems? Ask leading questions; you don't want yes or no answers.

- **Understand their behaviors and personality:** Assessment tools like Myers-Briggs, Wonderlic, and eSkill can help you peel back the layers and get a clearer picture of the type of employee they could potentially be.

Meet the Team

The transition of ownership can already be a perilous tightrope, and most experts agree that going in guns blazing on day one and implementing huge, sweeping changes isn't necessarily the best tactic. *(Unless you've got some real spoiled apples, then go ahead and toss those suckers out.)* Instead, approach it from a place of learning. Use this time to understand them and the business better. Ask them questions. What do they think the business does well? What suggestions do they have to improve the company? Give them an opportunity for buy-in. Lay out your vision and ask for their feedback. You may discover some underutilized talent… or realize a few more rotten apples need to be chucked.

Learn the Systems

What is the day-to-day flow like? Who are the vendors? Can you meet them? Do they have a playbook or standards of operations? If you can keep the original owner on as a consultant as part of the agreement, your operator (or you) should be spending all their time with them, learning and absorbing as much as possible. This kind of training is gold and can show you where the business shines and where improvements can be made.

Understand the Finances

Just as you would review your personal budget and finances regularly (at least, we hope you are), you should plan to review your new business budget and finances routinely. You should know exactly what's coming in and what's going out. Knowledge is power, after all. If you know what you have to work with, you know how many people you can hire, you know if you can afford the expansion, or you know if you can buy new equipment. **There's no forward movement without it.** Make it a weekly, bi-weekly, or monthly check-in...just make it consistent and stick to it!

Set Goals

This is no time to become complacent. What do you want to focus on? Where do you want to see the business grow? **Remember to make them SMART: Specific, Measurable, Achievable, Relevant, and Time-Bound.** From there, it's taking a look at each of them individually and deciding what you need to prioritize to meet those goals.

TAKE ACTION

Get out a sheet of paper and list your one-month, three-month, and 12-month **SMART** goals as they relate to your new business's finances, employees, systems, and operations. From there, assign each of them a priority level and make sure you're looking at these goals ***every.single.day.***

Chapter Two

I GET BY WITH A LITTLE HELP FROM MY COMPETITIVE ANALYSIS

THINK ABOUT IT:

"The time your game is most vulnerable is when you're ahead. Never let up."

- Rod Laver, Adidas

For most small business owners, the number one goal is Profitability. Without that, the lights don't stay on, the employees don't get paid, and operations will cease to exist (regardless of good intentions or a meaningful mission statement). Unless you're running a charity and depending on the kindness of strangers, the focus must remain on the bottom line.

One way you do this is by improving profit margins. (More to come on that in the next section.) But for now, we're going to talk about **Competitive Analysis.**

What is it?

Competitive analysis is the process of researching, assessing, and evaluating your competitor's weaknesses and strengths. It provides invaluable data and insight into what they're doing well or not so well.

Why is it important?

In the same way, you (should) analyze your own systems and processes to identify shortcomings and areas for improvement, the same technique can be used to gain a competitive edge over your competition. And when you know what they're up to and what you're up against, you have the upper hand.

How do I do a competitive analysis?

It sounds simple in theory but understand that the process itself can be time-consuming and even a little complicated. We know the day-to-day demands can be, well, frankly, *demanding*. And more often than not, it's more important to put the fires out in your own backyard rather than worrying about what's going on up the street. However, regular competitive analysis should be a priority if you want long-term success. The threat of competitors is a slow burn, but one that can still consume you all the same if you aren't ready for it.

To help you out, we have eight steps to get you started. All you need is a spreadsheet and time, and you're ready to go.

1. Identify your competitors

Start by making a list of every competitor you already know. After that, take it one step further and Google your business name. The search engine will happily supply a list of similar businesses you may or may not know about. Add them to the list.

2. Identify your indirect competitors

While they may offer services or products that differ from yours, they may still target the same market. For example, if you own a pet supply store, an indirect competitor could be a dog grooming business. Adding these to your analysis will provide more thorough insights into your market.

3. Review their products or services

Depending on the industry or type of business, you might find all you need online, or you may need to make discreet, in-person visits.

- What do they offer that's similar?
- What do they offer that's different?
- How does your pricing compare to similar products or services?

4. Check out their website

If you take the time to dig, there's a lot to be uncovered. In addition to reviewing prices and product descriptions, their website can offer insights. Do they push any particular product or service (often featured on the home page)? Do they have any upcoming events? Do they have links to media interviews? Check out their About Us or Mission Statement sections. Does anything stand out? How easy is the site to navigate?

5. Review their customer satisfaction

Check out their reviews on Google or Yelp for unfiltered feedback on why their customers love them and, more importantly, why they don't. Look for trends. Do they complain or praise their customer service? Are they satisfied with the quality? What about prices or shipping speeds?

6. Check out their social media

What platforms are they utilizing to connect with their customers? Do they offer tutorial videos on YouTube? Do they run contests and promotions on Facebook? Do they use influencers on Instagram? What kind of language are they using? How many followers do they have? Are they responding to comments or complaints?

7. How are they advertising?

Have you noticed their ads in local newspapers or radio stations? How about bus stop benches or billboards? Do they have an email list? (If so, definitely sign up! What could be easier than info on your competitors delivered right to your inbox?) What about ads on social media? (You know how it goes, once you search for something online, the magical compu-cookies will start showing you ads for that exact thing in mere minutes.)

8. Employ third-party analysis

Sites like SimilarWeb, Ubersuggest, Google Trends, or SpyFu to check relevant keywords in your niche, analyze website traffic sources and where your competitors are being mentioned, provide SEO-based tips and strategies, and much more. The best part is that a lot of them are completely free.

Bring it All Together Now

With your data in hand and more knowledge about the competition than you know what to do with, here comes the fun part. (Though that might be subjective.) All the time spent collecting is pointless if you don't sit down and actually analyze what you've uncovered and then use it as a measuring stick to see how you stack up. Here are some things you should be looking out for:

- How is your competition similar to one another? How is it different?
- On that note, what similarities do you share with your competition? And in what areas do you differ?
- Are prices for similar products and services standard across the board? Or do you see noticeable differences?
- Are they doing a better job utilizing social media?
- Is their website easier to navigate?
- Are they offering perks you aren't, like free shipping, bulk discounts, or reward programs?
- What weakness does the competition display? Do you have a solution to fulfill a need that they aren't?
- Where do you rank among the competition in search results? Who's higher?

Regular competitive analysis may seem daunting, but it's a strategy that will help you build long-term success. You might feel comfortable with your position in your market now but don't rest on your laurels. When you're ahead, you're vulnerable. That's when the target is on YOUR back, and everybody is comin' for ya. This is the way you stay one step ahead of them.

TAKE ACTION

This assignment is easy. ***Do exactly what we explained in detail above.*** Whether it's old-school graph paper (do they still make that?) or an Excel spreadsheet, don't put off the *very necessary* task of competitive analysis.

Chapter Three

PLEASE MIND YOUR MARGINS

THINK ABOUT IT:

"I'm convinced that about half of what separates the successful entrepreneurs from the non-successful ones is pure perseverance."

- Steve Jobs

If you want your business to be successful, it needs to be profitable. And if you want it to be profitable, you need to know and understand a little something called **profit margins**. After all, if you aren't bringing in money, the bills don't get paid, and that story, my friend, is one that never ends well.

In very simplified terms, a **profit margin** is a percentage of how much profit your business generates per dollar of sale. Example: If you have a 30% profit margin, it means you're netting $0.30 of income on every dollar.

To arrive at this percentage, start with your revenue and deduct the total cost of goods sold, expenses, interest, and taxes (Your net income). Divide that number by the original revenue amount, multiply by 100, and alakazam, you have your profit margin and a clear picture of how your business is fairing.

As a business owner, it's important that you get - and stay - very, very familiar with your profit margins. We're talking Tommy *Lee and Pam Anderson with a video camera*-familiar. There shouldn't be any secrets or surprises. Having this kind of familiarity will enable you to make wise and rational decisions when it comes to protecting the profitability and sustainability of your business, as well as course-correct when you see that percentage slipping. Your margins should act as a metric but also something you use to analyze and evaluate.

How can you improve profit margins?

Don't fall into the trap of thinking, *"if I just sell more, I'll be fine."* That might not actually be the real issue if you're hemorrhaging money elsewhere. Instead of just slapping a Band-Aid on the problem and praying it goes away, here are some useful tips to help you mind your margins.

- **Regularly reevaluate what you charge,** but don't jack up the prices for no reason. Yes, in theory, making customers pay more would give you a better profit margin, but it could have the opposite effect and drive them away. You may find you need to start charging more for legit reasons (looking at you, inflation) but make sure you do it strategically.
- When you're analyzing your prices, **consider what else you can offer that's of value** that could help justify the increase in the eyes of your customers.
- While you're at it, think about **upselling and cross-selling.** How can you increase your average order value?
- **What are you offering that has a low-profit margin?** If a particular product or service takes up a lot of time and energy and generates very little profit for your bottom line, consider pulling the plug if it can't be salvaged.
- **Reduce your overhead.** Can you work out of a smaller space? Can you renegotiate your lease agreement? What about your employees? We don't like to talk about letting people go, but tough decisions need to be made if it affects the bottom line.

Are there any tasks you can outsource rather than paying for them in-house?

- **Be militant about tracking your expenses.** You should know where every dollar and nickel are going - that's the only way you'll learn how and where to cut costs.
- **Renegotiate your contracts with vendors.** See if they'll offer discounts for purchasing in bulk or extending the length of your contracts. It never hurts to ask, right?
- **Focus on efficiency, streamline your operation, and reduce waste.** Sometimes it comes down to throwing out the playbook and making a new one. If you can deliver the same product or service in a more efficient and less wasteful manner, your profit margins will reflect that. Just don't cut corners and sacrifice quality in the name of the almighty dollar. Your customers will notice.

Bottom line

Big, sweeping changes aren't always necessary to improve your profit margins. Some of the examples we shared above will require a bit more legwork than others but instituting one or two of these can significantly impact your bottom line. Minding your margins should be a regular practice if you're serious about growing and sustaining your business.

TAKE ACTION

When's the last time you truly (*truly* - no cheating now) took a long, hard look at your Profit Margins? If it's been a minute, **this is your sign to move it to the top of your To Do list.** Compare your findings to other organizations in your industry to see how you stack up. If you don't like what you're seeing, we just gave you eight ways you can turn things around.

Chapter Four

DON'T STOP ME NOW: HOW TO ADD VALUE TO YOUR BUSINESS

THINK ABOUT IT:

"When you stop growing, you start dying."

- William S. Burroughs

This cheerful little quip is a poignant reminder for small business owners that becoming stagnant isn't an option if you want to be successful. And that's the goal, right? If you want to create long-term success - not to mention survive the competition - you can't rest on your laurels or settle for the status quo. You need to be proactive.

One of the ways you can do this is by increasing the value of your business. This can lead to better profit margins, happier employees, more satisfied customers, and scalability - which means you can continue operating for years to come (or at least as long as you'd like).

You can add value to your business in various ways, some of which are entirely free while others require a bit more time or money. Below we've listed seven areas you can focus on right now to get started.

Review the Current SOPs

Standard Operating Procedures (SOPs), when done well, are detailed instructions on how to carry out any job or task within the company that any employee can follow. Designed to standardize the most efficient and cost-effective means to achieve the desired outcome, SOPs make it easier to train new employees, delegate tasks, and keep operations running smoothly. In short, they're a playbook for success. But they aren't a one-and-done. Whether it's a company you've just acquired or one you've been running for years, periodic reviews of its SOPs can help you identify areas of improvement.

Improve the Quality of Your Products or Services

You can't just slap on some higher ticket prices and call it a day. Sure, your revenue will probably go up for the time being, but it's not a sustainable solution for long-term growth and success. You either need to offer a better quality of product or service to justify the increase - - or be a real good snail-oil touting shyster. (For the record, we support the first one.) Look for ways you can add value and quality that your customers will *want* to pay more for.

Invest in Your Employees

The right employees can make or break your business. If they align with your company values, believe in the product or service, and are invested in the overall success of the business, they're only going to add value to your overall operation. Unhappy, unsuited, poorly-trained, and poorly incentivized employees will obviously have the opposite effect. Invest time and resources into your team through incentive or reward programs, management training, or professional skill development. (The same goes for you solo-flyers! Invest in yourself as well. You're the only employee you have!)

Improve Customer Service

How can your customers reach you? How accessible is someone from your team to answer questions or address complaints? Do they wait days for a return call? Are they greeted by an unfriendly and unbothered call center clerk after-hours? Is your contact information readily available on your website? Think about the businesses you frequent and compare how their CS stacks up against your own. Even if you royally effed up, good customer service can go a long, long way to salvage the situation. Happy customers = happy reviews = more customers = more money = more value.

Listen to Your Customers

Similar to the point right above, but different enough that it deserves its own paragraph. Small businesses have a significant advantage over Big Box Chains because they communicate more directly with their customers and can be better attuned to their needs. That's huge! Ask for feedback, send out surveys, heck -- chat 'em up while they're at the cash register. This is golden info at your fingertips. Don't assume you know what they want. The business owners who listen - and give - the people what they ask for will always come out ahead.

Invest in Technology

Let us clarify - invest in GOOD technology. If you spend half your day resetting the routers, unjamming the printers, calling IT, or doing anything else for an unreasonable amount of time that could have been solved easily with updated equipment or tech, please make that a priority. It can be a costly investment but well worth the headache it saves you - - not to mention the time you'll get back to put into other more worthwhile pursuits.

Become an Expert

This isn't something that will happen overnight - but becoming an expert in your field, and earning that reputation, will increase your business's value exponentially. Whether it's through studying the market, analyzing trends, attending conferences on the latest updates in your industry, taking online courses, spending time on the production line, making deliveries, answering the phones, or a little bit of everything - the more time you spend getting to know all the pieces of the puzzle (even if you suck with the execution of one of those pieces) you'll have a better understanding of the full picture. You gotta know how the sausage gets made, so to speak. Then show off that expertise by publishing to your website's blog or social media accounts to reach more people and potential customers.

Taking the time and intentionally adding value to your business is one of the best investments you can make for long-term growth.

TAKE ACTION

Bonus 10: Grab your free copy of our **8 Ways to Grow Your Business Worksheet.**

Chapter Five

THE REASON NOBODY HAS EVER HEARD OF YOU

THINK ABOUT IT:

"Rarely have I seen a situation where doing less than the other guy is a good strategy."
- Jimmy Spithill

Picture it. You have a swell idea or product that could turn the world on its head and put a stop to climate change, end world hunger, and bring peace to the Middle East. *Where do we sign?*

Don't start writing your Nobel Peace Prize acceptance speech quite yet, friend. Because at the end of the day, it doesn't matter how good the idea is if nobody knows (or cares) about it.

Enter Brand Awareness.

What is it?

Brand awareness is simply what makes people aware of your very existence and helps set you apart from your competitors. It's your opportunity to present your products or services in such a way that makes them easily recognizable to customers, as well as **establish your authority or expertise.**

Why is it important?

It establishes trust with your customers and influences their decision-making processes. The better brand awareness you have, the more valuable your business is. *Cha-ching!* When you think of dish soap or sneakers or search engines, are you thinking of these in generic terms? Or did your mind immediately go to Dawn, Nike, and Google? That's the power of brand awareness.

How do you increase brand awareness?

Brand awareness is a beast that needs constant feeding and constant attention. If you're on a tight budget, the good news is that it can be so much more than just throwing money at advertising campaigns. While companies with more money may have an easier time of it, there are plenty of creative strategies you can implement that are cost-efficient (and sometimes free!) to increase your brand awareness. Here are seven ideas you can use to help get your creative juices flowing!

Brand Standards. You need to have a consistent identity across all platforms to be recognizable. (Signage, business cards, logos, social media, etc.) Pick a few complimentary fonts, select a color scheme, and stick with it. It might seem like an inconsequential thing, but it's just one part of the larger story you're telling about yourself and your business. If you can't hire a design expert, Canva.com has thousands of templates, logos, and color pallets to choose from, and the platform is very beginner-friendly.

Website. You have to have a website, hard stop. It doesn't need to be fancy. It doesn't need to have a ton of bells and whistles. What it *does need* is to look professional, be easy to navigate, and be simple for visitors to find what they're looking for. At the very least, you need Contact Information and an About page; this lets people know who they're potentially getting into business with. Of course, you can do much,

much more with a website, but if you're just starting out - start with the basics, and you can always add on from there. Sites like Wix and Squarespace are free and easy website builders that you can set up in just a few minutes.

Email Marketing. There's no easier (or more cost-efficient) way to stay connected with your current customers and reach a new audience than through regular email newsletters. You can drop into their inbox anytime you want with a quick update, promotion, product announcement, customer reviews, educational resources, and more.

Social Media. Love it or hate it, social media is here to stay; you might as well use it to your advantage. With 3.78 billion users and 54% of them using social media [5]to research products, it's a no-brainer. Don't feel like you have to do them all - at least not right away. Find the platform that resonates the most with you, then use it to regularly post ***valuable content*** that shows customers what you offer.

Freebies. Everyone loves free stuff! (And if they say they don't, they're lying.) Your brand can be put on almost anything nowadays, like pens, hats, Frisbees, socks, stickers, travel mugs, keychains, etc. They're great to have on hand for community events - and it's an automatic advertisement every time someone wears or uses that product in public. Freebies can apply to digital products as well. Consider providing a free e-book or access to a private Facebook group in exchange for their email address. Not only are you establishing your authority and giving them something of value, but you can also keep them engaged and reinforce your brand through future email marketing. Win-win!

Influencer Marketing. People love getting recommendations for products or services. Don't believe us? According to SproutSocial,[6] approximately 68% of consumers have made purchases because of social media influencers. If you can partner with people who have a large social

---

[5] Heitman, Stephanie. "174 Social Media Statistics & Facts That Just Might Blow Your Mind." LocaliQ. August 31, 2022.

[6] "Behaviors in the Social Shopping Cart." Sprout Social.

following - especially if they're already perceived as an expert - they can do wonders to increase and promote your brand awareness.

Podcasts. Podcasts have exploded in popularity over the last several years, with new shows getting added every single day in countless niches and industries. Starting your own podcast is a great way to get your message out, connect with others, and establish your brand and authority. If the idea feels overwhelming, consider being a guest on podcasts instead. Sites like Podmatch can help you connect and get booked on shows to reach a variety of audiences.

TAKE ACTION

Brand awareness is all about creating a narrative that establishes your business as an authority or expert in your industry or niche. Don't worry about doing all of these at once. **Start with the one that seems easiest to tackle first, then keep adding on;** there is no deadline or timetable - instead, it's a fluid process that will continue to evolve and change over time.

Chapter Six

SELLING IN THE ETHER: WHY ALL BUSINESSES SHOULD BE ONLINE

THINK ABOUT IT:

"Make your product easier to buy than your competition, or you will find your customers buying from them, not you."
- Mark Cuban

(PSA: Whether you own an e-commerce site, a brick-and-mortar store, or thinking of buying either one…this section is for you!)

E-commerce is a booming industry with no signs of slowing down. According to Statista[7], sales in 2021 amounted to approximately 4.9 trillion U.S. dollars worldwide - and it's **forecasted to grow another 50% over the next four years.** That's a lot of money, but it shouldn't come as much of a surprise. Just think how easy it is these days to buy online. Offers get delivered to our inboxes on the daily, targeted ads pop up when we scroll Instagram, Amazon has been waving that dangerous Order Now button for some time, and with Google Pay, we don't even need to get up to dig out our credit card when it's time to check out. **It's**

[7] Chevalier, Stephanie. "Retail e-commerce sales worldwide from 2014 to 2026." Statista. September 21, 2022.

so popular that many brick-and-mortar stores have pivoted to make their services and products accessible for online purchases.

If you are already involved in an e-commerce business, you're undoubtedly aware of the massive potential to generate sales - while equally aware of the massive amounts of competition. Good news travels fast, and every Tom, Dick, and Harry is looking to get a cut of those trillions of dollars. (Who can blame them, really?)

So, the question becomes, how do you carve out space within your niche to target consumers you want to turn into customers? The good news/bad news is there are a million different ways to approach this. Good, because there's a lot of revenue potential and paths to explore. Bad because those paths are more like a labyrinth with rules and trends that are constantly changing.

For example, Facebook ads are a very popular and lucrative tool for business owners to reach their audience. The downside is that Facebook makes all the rules AND changes all the rules, AND it can become a full-time job just to keep up with what works and what doesn't work to ensure your ads are optimized for peak performance. If you have the budget and are getting a good ROI (Return on Investment), it can be absolutely worth it.

But what if you don't have the budget? ***Or what if you don't want to put all your eggs in Mark Zuckerburg's Meta basket?*** (You'll want some eggs in there, just not all. Let us not forget that fateful day a few years back when the site was down for six long hours. Surveyed small business owners estimated they lost anywhere from a few hundred dollars to 5,000 dollars in revenue because of it.) [8]

Just like multiple revenue streams are important to growing wealth, having multiple access points to reach your customers is important to

---

[8] Subin, Samantha. "Facebook's outage has people rethinking how they make money online." CNBC. October 9, 2021.

grow a business. **(Even if you DON'T have an e-commerce business, you can still use many of these methods to reach people.)**

That may include:

- Email and Customer Lists
- Facebook pages or groups
- Instagram accounts
- Networking groups and masterminds
- Amazon listings
- Websites and landing pages
- Podcasts
- E-commerce sites

The catch is (there's always a catch) that many of these require a significant amount of time and sweat equity before you begin getting any type of ROI (Return on Investment). Building an email list takes time. Building an active Facebook group takes time. Gaining Instagram followers or Podcast subscribers or building a website with high traffic all takes time and energy.

Rather than building it from the ground up, what if we approached it the same way we've approached small business ownership? **Instead of building it...what if we buy it?**

Think of each item we listed above as an asset on the market available for purchase. Someone else has already put in the work to make it lucrative, and now you have the opportunity to capitalize on it. Someone who owns a dog grooming franchise would find an active *We <3 Dogs* Facebook group is very beneficial. If you sell supplements, purchasing an Instagram account within that niche (like fitness, diet, health, etc.) would give you instant access to thousands, even millions, of followers. A mortgage company would have a field day with a realtor's contact list. And so forth.

Keeping with this mindset, you can **now approach the acquisition of these assets in the same way you would approach a "traditional"**

business. What is its value? Why do they want to sell, and what is their motivation? What can you bring to the table? How can you make this a win-win for both parties? And finally, what creative funding strategies can you use to finance the deal? A traditional bank loan or SBA 7(a) loan probably wouldn't work, but what about Seller Financing? Or an Equity Earn-In Approach? Be willing to think outside the box and get creative!

Heraclitus said it best, "*there is nothing permanent except change.*" **And as business owners, the need to adapt and pivot is critical for growth and longevity.** What worked five or ten years ago may not be doing you any favors today. I mean, who would have thought that dancing TikTok clips would have quite the impact they do? Don't be afraid of change - embrace it and use it to your advantage. You may be surprised where it takes you.

TAKE ACTION

Take another look at the list above. Over the next few weeks, pause your Netflix account and **pick one** *(just one!)* **thing off this list, and see how you can adapt it to suit your purposes.** Most of them are FREE, and if it means more people walking through your doors (figuratively or literally), well, it's damn well worth it.

Chapter Seven

NEED A HAND? HOW TO SUCCESSFULLY OUTSOURCE FOR SUCCESS

THINK ABOUT IT:

"It's simple arithmetic: Your income can grow only to the extent that you do."

- T. Harv Eker

Running a business can be expensive and time-consuming—especially when you're first starting out or operating a one-man (or one-woman) show. Hiring full-time or even part-time help may be out of the question, but you know that if you want to grow and scale your business, something has to give.

The concept of outsourcing has grown in popularity over the years, both for its time-saving and money-saving benefits. Recent statistics show that 37% [9]of small businesses outsource at least part of their process to focus on their core business, improve the quality of service, solve capacity issues, or meet their business needs. Even big-name companies like Peloton are outsourcing production as a way to cut costs.

[9] Samantha. "Outsourcing Statistics 2022: In the US and Globally." TeamStage.

If you're ready to start outsourcing for success but have questions on the hows, whys, and logistics of it all, keep reading.

What Should I Outsource?

This is obviously the first question you should be asking yourself. Take a look at the tasks and projects on your to-do list.

- Is there anything that you aren't particularly good at?
- Is there anything that is taking up a lot of your time?
- Is there anything that doesn't need your personal involvement to be completed?

If you're a financial whiz but can only muster up mediocre copy, why not outsource to someone who has a flair for the written word?

If you spend a lot of time answering customer emails or responding to inquiries, why not outsource those tasks to a Virtual Assistant and give yourself some time back to focus on big picture tasks?

Yes, you could probably teach yourself how to build a website (you can learn anything on YouTube these days), but millions of people already have that skill set and expertise who can help develop and manage a professional-looking site on your behalf.

Hate social media but recognize the importance of having an online presence? Outsource. Don't have time to balance the books? Outsource. Do you lack the space or workforce to ship your products? Outsource to a drop shipping service.

The bottom line is you can outsource nearly anything and everything. Time is money. Paying someone for something you could potentially do yourself might seem counterproductive, but your time is valuable. And by freeing yourself from the weight of more mundane tasks, you can focus your thoughts and energy on building and growing your business - which is the goal!

How Do I Get Started?

You don't have to outsource everything at once. In fact, it's probably **best to start small** and then gradually delegate more and more tasks. If you need help with web design, copywriting, and accounting, you're likely going to need three separate individuals who excel in those specific niches. This means you have to find, screen, interview, and (to a degree) train three people to take those tasks on. That's a lot to handle simultaneously.

Start with your most pressing need first. Then crunch the numbers and **set a budget** for what you can realistically pay to outsource the project to someone.

Next, create your project description. **This is one of the most critical parts of the outsourcing process.** You need a detailed, clear description of the project and defined goals and expectations. How can you expect an outsider to know if you yourself don't know what those things are?

Where Do I Find People to Outsource To?

- Ask people you know. Maybe someone in your professional circle is a web designer or videographer or analyzes corporations for a living. They might be looking for a side hustle (who isn't these days?) or could point you to someone who is.
- Use a Third-Party Site. This is the most straightforward direction to go. Many websites can help match you with the right freelancer, including Fiverr, Upwork, DesignCrowd, Dribble, and FlexJobs.

How Do I Know If They're the Right Person for the Job?

Screening and vetting the right fit can be a time-consuming process. Some sites will allow you to search profiles based on ratings, experience, costs, niches, etc. Other sites will allow you to request services, and freelancers can send you bids for the project.

As you begin the selection process, whether online or through your own network, here are a few things to keep in mind:

- Pay attention to **Ratings** and **Reviews**: How satisfied have other buyers been with their work? This is a pretty good indication of what you can expect if you work with them. Did they deliver on time? Did they provide the expected service? What, if any, were the negatives of working with this individual?
- Check out their **portfolio**. If they don't have one, ask for samples. This likely won't apply to hiring a Virtual Assistant or Accountant, but for things like web designers or copywriters, **you should absolutely take a look at their past work** to see if it meets your standards.
- Don't sacrifice quality. **You get what you pay for.** Yes, be smart about it (that's why you established a budget in the first place) but don't take the first cheap offer that comes along, especially if it's too good to be true. Someone who is severely undercharging compared to their colleagues is undercharging for a reason.
- **Make sure they understand the project description.** Have they worked on similar projects in the past? How long have they worked in the industry? Can they meet the deadline? Do they have specific working hours when they can be reached? Invite them to ask questions. (The good ones will.) **Remember, you're looking for someone to make your life easier, not add to your responsibilities.** You may want to look elsewhere if you sense they will need a lot of handholding and support (beyond what's expected at the beginning of a new project).
- **Compare, compare, compare!** Don't just pick the first person who checks off the boxes because you're in a hurry to delegate the project to someone else. **Review at least 5-10 candidates**. How do they stack up against each other? Compare prices, experience, portfolios, and even your conversations with them.

Final Thoughts

Outsourcing is a great approach to help you grow and scale your business. But it is an investment and should be approached as such. You are not only investing money, but you are also investing time and energy into finding, vetting, and supporting the right people to help you meet your goals.

TAKE ACTION

Bonus 11: Listen to **How to Find, Hire, and Manage Filipino Virtual Workers with John Jonas: Episode 47 of The Liquid Lunch Project Podcast.**

John Jonas is the founder of OnlineJobs.ph, a job board for finding virtual workers in the Philippines. If you've tried outsourcing before and had little luck, give it another go. John's teachings will certainly impact the way you think about operating your business, outsourcing, and the level of success you may achieve.

Chapter Eight

THE SUCCESSFUL BUSINESS TRIFECTA: EMPLOYEES, CUSTOMERS, AND CUSTOMER SERVICE

THINK ABOUT IT:

"The difference between a boss and a leader: a boss says 'Go!' - a leader says, 'Let's go!'"

- E.M. Kelly

All businesses have many moving parts and pieces that contribute to or detract from their overall success. Profit margins, supply chain and inventory issues, customer relations, inflation, funding, cash flow, and competition are just the tip of the iceberg.

If you don't want to sail a sinking ship, you need to keep your ear to the ground (or deck, maybe?) on each and every one of these. But for today, we're going to focus on three areas that are all interconnected and can significantly impact your business -- for good or for bad.

Finding Customers.
Recruiting and Retaining Dedicated Employees.
Developing Good Customer Service.

- For a business to grow, you need to **attract more customers.**
- More customers mean you need to **hire more employees** to keep up with the demand.
- More demand means more **employee and customer interactions.**
- More interactions mean more opportunities for employees to **provide excellent (or not so excellent) customer service.**
- Excellent customer service means **more customers are coming to your door.**
- More customers mean...*well, you get the idea.*

They are like the wheels on a tricycle; each one depends on the others to stay upright. You can have fantastic employees and great customer service, but that only works if you have the customers. Your marketing could be working like gangbusters, but if you don't have the employees to meet the demand, you're not going to get very far.

Continue reading for a closer look at each of these "wheels" and the actionable steps you can start today.

Finding Customers

Every business, no matter the size, wants to attract new customers. That's why companies shell out insane amounts of green to get their message into consumers' faces. *(Just look at the going rate for a 30-second spot at the 2023 Superbowl. Got $7 million to spare?)* But for smaller businesses that don't have the same amount of cash and resources to devote to marketing and advertising, how do they reach new customers?

<u>**Action Steps:**</u>

- **Ask for referrals.** Use customer loyalty to your advantage and ask them to recommend your products or services to friends. You can even set up a reward system for extra incentivization.

- **Reconnect with previous customers.** Their reasons for separating may vary, but it's worth reaching out to see if circumstances have changed or to apprise them of any new updates or offers they might be interested in.
- **Attend community events.** The late Queen famously said, "I have to be seen to be believed." Get your face out there and start connecting with the community you serve.
- **Update your website.** A frequent way customers discover new businesses is through an online search. It's a crowded space, and if you want to stand out, make sure your site is easy to find, easy to navigate, and clearly identifies what you do and how to reach you.

Recruiting and Retaining Dedicated Employees

Having the right team in place can make all the difference for your business's success (not to mention your sanity). But finding, hiring, training, AND keeping good employees can be pretty challenging. A revolving door makes it difficult to operate and scale; it's like trying to brush your teeth with a mouthful of Oreos -- it just keeps getting worse.

<u>Action Steps:</u>

- **Describe your ideal employee.** What skills would you like them to have? What qualities should they possess? You don't need to make it a black-and-white issue, but this will at least provide some clarity on the type of person you would like to hire.
- **Spend time on your job ads.** Don't go generic for the sake of time. Your job ads should be well thought out, detailed, and specific to the role you're trying to fill. Jeff Brekken (owner and founder of Blue Sky Benefits Solutions) recommends placing employer questions within the job itself -- and if an applicant hasn't bothered to answer them, their resume automatically goes into the trash. This can save you a lot of time sorting through applications of people who can't follow simple instructions. (Listen to our entire conversation with Jeff over on the Liquid Lunch Project podcast.)

- **Train your employees.** Once you have hired the right person for the job, train them well. You probably didn't bring a mind reader onto your staff, so take the time to provide training, support, and clear communication of your goals and expectations.
- **Create and improve your SOPs.** When was the last time you looked at or updated your Standard Operating Procedures? Your employees will be more successful if they have standardized processes they can follow that clearly explain every aspect of their job and responsibilities.
- **Invest in your employees.** That revolving door we mentioned can be pretty expensive, so retaining your employees and keeping them happy and satisfied with their work will pay huge dividends in the long run. Obviously, more money in the paycheck is always a popular choice, but you can also offer flexible scheduling options, reward them with extra days off, provide mentorship, give public kudos for a job well done, cover a portion of their health insurance, or give them buy-in to the company.

Developing Good Customer Service

One of the advantages or disadvantages (depending on how you want to look at it) of the digital age is that everyone's opinions on anything and everything can live in perpetuity online. That's great if you've made someone happy, but customers will not hesitate to put you on blast if they're unsatisfied with any aspect of your business. The best way to mitigate these scenarios is to ensure you and your team provide top-notch customer service.

Action Steps:

- **Be proactive, not reactive.** Don't wait to address customer concerns or complaints after the grievance has been aired. You'll have a much harder time salvaging the relationship. Instead, a simple follow-up to ask if they're satisfied with the service or product they received can go a long way and can help you fix any problems before it goes public.

- **Be accessible.** How easily can your customers reach you if they have a concern? Can your contact information be found online? When they call in, do they have to wait through a long list of prompts to get them to the correct department? (Which, let's face it, will only add to their displeasure.) Consider simplifying the process so they can speak with someone more quickly. Set up an auto-reply email that lets them know their message has been received and how soon they can expect a response.
- **Develop your communication skills.** In a past episode of The Liquid Lunch Project podcast, our guest Brenden from MasterTalk asked our listeners when was the last time they thought about their communication goals. Every time you interact with someone is an opportunity to grow your business -- so it's crazy that we don't spend more time and energy developing this skill.

Just like a tricycle, you can't rely on or depend on just one wheel. (That's called a unicycle and a very different riding experience.) Your business needs to focus on all three simultaneously to truly achieve long-term sustainability and success.

TAKE ACTION

Bonus 12: Listen to **The Poster Boy of Disruption with Terry Jones: Episode 28 of The Liquid Lunch Project Podcast.**

Terry Jones, **founder of Travelocity.com,** has been called the poster boy of disruption. In this episode, he discusses the importance of staying curious, what you can be - and should be - learning from other industries, how to hire the best people for the job, and he used tech to disrupt the travel industry.

Chapter Nine

DIDN'T SEE THAT ONE COMING: THE UNEXPECTED COSTS OF OWNING A BUSINESS

THINK ABOUT IT:

"By failing to prepare, you are preparing to fail."
- Benjamin Franklin

Unexpected costs when running a business are going to pop up at the worst possible time (think *giant zit right before the big high school dance* kind of timing). It doesn't matter how carefully and thoroughly you planned your budget – Murphy's Law guarantees the one expense you didn't account for is the one you're going to incur.

With that in mind, today, we're going to cover five unexpected costs you might encounter as a business owner. It's our way of giving you the upper hand…and giving ole Murphy the middle digit.

Equipment Failure & Maintenance

Nothing lasts forever, and at some point, everything from construction equipment, machinery, ovens, printers, and computers will need servicing or replaced altogether. Depending on the nature of your business, some of these will immediately negatively impact your bottom line. (If you have a print shop and your printers go up, you're in trouble.)

Consider This: What equipment is vital to keep your operation running? Make sure you have an emergency fund or access to capital to cover those costs.

Employees

More employees (hopefully) mean business is good, and you need additional support to serve your customers. And while they might be helping you bring in more money, it also means you're putting out more money. It's not just wages; you should also account for the costs that come with hiring, training, taxes, and offering benefits.

Consider This: Reviewing and negotiating insurance options on an annual basis, focusing on employee retention through non-monetary incentives (see our post here for some ideas), and having a "*fire fast, hire slow*" approach to bring new people onto the team can help cut down on your overall expenses.

Payment Processing Fees

Who uses cash anymore? (Maybe Timmy for his roadside lemonade stand, but even then, his mom probably has a Venmo account as a backup.) Every day we are one step closer to a cashless society, and while that makes it more convenient for both buyer and seller, it also comes with additional costs. Those small percentage fees that credit card vendors or Point of Sales systems charge may not seem like a lot, but they add up quickly – especially for small business owners.

Consider This: Do a little research and analysis to determine how much of your revenue is going to the process of collecting payment. See if there's any room for negotiation. (The worst they can say is no.) You could also think about adding a surcharge to offset the cost (if your state allows it) or offer ACH payments, as they are much less expensive for a business to accept.

Supplies & Inventory

There are myriad ways you can incur unexpected costs in this category - especially if you're providing a tangible product. First and foremost, the price of raw materials to make your product – or the product's cost- can change dramatically. That means you must decide whether you can afford to eat the extra expense or pass that on to your customers (and potentially lose out on sales.)

Additionally, inventory can be damaged or stolen, so even though you bought (and planned to sell) 100 custom-made bird baths, if three of them broke during the unloading process, you now only have 97 you can make money off of. (FYI: Having fewer items in stock than recorded in the inventory books is referred to as "*shrinkage*" and has nothing to do with that Seinfeld episode.)

Consider This: Obviously, be careful when handling inventory, so you don't wind up with unusable bird baths. Evaluate your own prices for wiggle room in the event you need to raise them. Beyond that, make sure you're regularly reviewing the costs of supplies and goods. Negotiate if you're able or look at alternative suppliers.

Professional Services

You might fancy yourself a one-stop shop for everything your business needs to operate, but the truth of the matter is, you're not - *nor should you be.* It's that whole "Jack of all trades, master of none" bit. You can't expect yourself to be an authority on everything from payroll to taxes to legal matters or IT. Sometimes you'll need to call in the professionals – and they will want to be compensated.

Consider This: Be proactive and make room in the budget so you can call on their help when you need it. The good news is that even though you are paying them for their services, they're really saving you money in the long run because, as experts, they will (hopefully) do it right the first time – unlike yourself, who may spend an excessive amount of time and energy trying to figure it out on your own.

You can't prepare for everything - but you can plan ahead. Keep these expenses on your radar, continuously evaluate what you're spending your money on, shop around for better policies and terms, speak to a financial expert, and focus on beefing up an emergency fund or getting access to capital to help with the unexpected. Every little bit helps.

TAKE ACTION

Over the next few weeks, your assignment is to go through this list one by one and determine how you can prepare for each of these potential **problems - and then put a game plan in action.** You'll thank us later.

Chapter Ten

OUR SECOND FAVORITE F-WORD: FREE RESOURCES TO GROW & SCALE YOUR BUSINESS

THINK ABOUT IT:

"There is only one success - to be able to spend your life in your own way."
- Christopher Morley

Funding may be our favorite F-word, but FREE comes in at a pretty close second.

When you're operating a small business, every penny counts - especially if you have razor-thin margins. This can make it a challenge to scale and grow your business if you don't have extra funds sitting around to hire experts or purchase fancy equipment or software.

The good news is that there are plenty of absolutely 100% free programs and resources that can help you achieve your goals without spending one solitary cent. And as an added bonus, many of them will also save you time. (And we all know time is money, so win-win.)

Here are eight free resources you can use to help manage and scale your small business.

Calendly

A personal favorite of ours, Calendly is one of the best online scheduling tools out there by eliminating the hassle of back-and-forth emails when trying to get an appointment on the books. Its user-friendly hub is a breeze to set up and can be customized for your availability preferences, meeting type, and questionnaire forms. Plus, it integrates with your favorite calendars and tools, and you can embed it into your website for streamlined scheduling. Perfect for people in sales, marketing, recruitment, IT, and more.

Avast

If ANY part of your business operates on the World Wide Web (think website, banking, etc.), your data is vulnerable to scammers and hackers. Avast is an award-winning free virus protection program you can download with just a click on your PC, Mac, Android, or iPhone. It safeguards your home network, has six layers of security, stops ransomware threats, and blocks distractions and interruptions, all without slowing down your device.

Slack

Collaboration in the time of Covid prompted many businesses to find a solution to the challenge of working together as a team when not physically sharing the same space. One of the most popular platforms to rise from the ashes, so to speak, is Slack. It works for all types of companies and industries to connect with different members of your teams by sharing files, sending audio and video clips, and having real-time communication via chat or a live huddle.

Coursera

Any business owner or entrepreneur worth their salt knows that the quest for knowledge is a never-ending journey. But you don't need to shell out big bucks or enroll in an accredited program in pursuit of education. **Coursera** has an impressive number of entirely free courses on topics ranging from financial markets, statistics, psychology, brand management, negotiation strategies, venture capital, and more.

DocuSign

Fax machines - and even printers - are slowly going the way of the dinosaurs, making collecting signatures a bit of a challenge. Bypass this roadblock by sending your documents via DocuSign. It's super simple to use and lets you collect necessary signatures anytime, anyplace. The free edition allows you to sign as many documents as you want and keeps everything secure in cloud storage for easy access.

Canva

If you need simple graphics and don't have the money to hire a professional, Canva's free version might just be your new best friend. With plenty of pre-designed templates to select from, you can create social media posts, flyers, logos, and more with just a few clicks of the mouse. You get more features to play around with as part of the paid version, but the free plan has everything you need for basic designs.

Bplans

Do you need help writing your business plan? Bplans has over 500 real-world examples from a variety of industries that can help guide you through the process. Select from categories like "Accounting, Insurance & Compliance," "Children & Pets," or "Entertainment & Recreation" - all completely free.

Wave

Touted as one-stop money management for small business owners, Wave software helps you to invoice clients, track expenses and income, and simplify your receipts come tax season. You can also accept payments on a pay-per-use basis and process payroll for a monthly fee. With free unlimited bank and credit card connections and access to helpful reports like *Overdue Invoices & Bills* and *Profit & Loss*, Wave can be a useful tool to have in your small business arsenal.

TAKE ACTION

You get a ***free*** pass today. (*See what we did there?*) Depending on where you're at in your business or even the type of business you're in, you might not need any of these free resources…yet. Keep this information in the back of your mind. You never know when you'll wish you had them!

Chapter Eleven

DO YOU SMELL SOMETHING BURNING? HOW TO AVOID ENTREPRENEUR BURNOUT

THINK ABOUT IT:

"You've got to get up every morning with determination if you're going to go to bed with satisfaction."

- George Lorimer

Burnout: exhaustion of physical or emotional strength or motivation, usually as a result of prolonged stress or frustration

If you're an entrepreneur or small business owner, you probably don't need the dictionary definition of the word; it's a reality you're all too familiar with. Starting a business -- and keeping it operational -- is no small feat. Elon Musk describes it as *"eating glass and staring into the abyss. If you go into expecting that it's going to be just fun, you're going to be disappointed. It's not. It's quite painful."*

Cheery, right?

So, why do people do it? **What makes entrepreneurs take the long, hard path with no shortcuts and no guaranteed success?** Why the hell would someone choose to take "the road less traveled" when there are plenty of other safer, less tumultuous options out there? I know Robert Frost claimed it made all the difference, but to what end?

Because you want something more. Because you don't want to settle. Because you're crazy enough to believe that if you want something bad enough, you can get it.

And so, you get it -- and do what so many other people cannot. (*We raise a glass.*) But there is a price to pay, and often the cost is your own health and well-being. **That doesn't have to be your story.**

Like most things in life, it's all about balance. You don't need to sacrifice your goals -- or yourself. You can have yourself a big 'ole slice of chocolate cake and eat it, too. (Maybe with a nice glass of red?) **To help you achieve that balance, here are some of our favorite tips to avoid entrepreneur burnout.**

Delegate

Stop treating delegation as a dirty word. The old "*if you want something done right, you have to do it yourself*" attitude isn't going to win you any trophies for the mantle. If you're still in one-person operation mode, consider outsourcing some of your work and get your time back. **It can still be done right if you find the right person for the job.**

Exercise

You don't need to start training for the New York City Marathon or anything, but doing just 30 minutes of some sort of physical activity every day can significantly improve your mood, give you more energy, help you sleep better, and combat anxiety and depression. (Yes, even *that kind* of physical activity.) **Did you know that 7% of the general population suffers from depression, but 30% of entrepreneurs do?** That right there is enough reason to lace up the tennis shoes and get moving.

Unplug

IT Lesson 101: If something isn't working, try unplugging it for a few minutes. The same goes for people. Humans are tied to technology like never before, and if you're running a business, you're probably connected to it more than most. (Except for those professional gamers, but that's a whole other level.) **We were not created to live hunched over glowing blue screens or consuming and processing an impossible amount of information coming from all corners of the globe.** Put the phone down. Step away from the computer screen. Turn off your notifications for a while. Keep Saturday's social media free. Whatever you need to do to unplug yourself on a regular basis, do it.

Set Office Hours

It's easy to fall into an (unhealthy) rhythm of working around the clock. **Businesses and enterprises just starting out certainly need more attention, but the 24/7 grind isn't a sustainable lifestyle**. Maybe you don't actually *need* to be in problem-solving mode all the time or immediately respond to every email, message, or phone call. *Perish the thought!* (But it's true.) Boundaries are a good thing -- give it a try sometime. Create your own office hours (you're the boss, after all) and work when it's time to work. And when the proverbial whistle blows, slide down the dinosaur back ala Fred Flintstone style, and call it a day. The routine and the break will be Yabba-Dabba-good.

Prioritize

Some days, it feels like everything is on fire, no? But the truth is -- it probably isn't. It just feels that way because you're looking at all your projects and to-dos as one enormous task you have to tackle. **Before you jump feet-first into problem-solving mode, take five or ten minutes and write down everything you need to do in the next eight or so hours.** (Ditch the Notes App and go old school with paper and pen. It's proven to keep you more engaged and helps with memory.) Then give the list a good once over like your Tim Gunn on Project Runway. **Underline what's important. Highlight what's urgent.** If a task is *BOTH*, those are your number one priorities. The things that are either underlined *OR* highlighted are priority number two. And anything on your list that's not gotten any lovin' can wait at the bottom of the totem pole (or be *cough cough* outsourced or delegated). Suddenly your big flaming mess of a day doesn't seem so unmanageable, eh? Like Tim says, *make it work*.

Avoiding entrepreneur burnout is all about setting healthy boundaries, learning to prioritize self-care, and managing the expectations you put on yourself. **For those who want it bad enough, the sky really is the limit** -- but you'll never get there if you're working yourself into an early grave.

TAKE ACTION

Bonus 13: Listen to **How to Run a Business Without it Running You with Richard Shaull: Episode 44 of The Liquid Lunch Project Podcast.**

Richard Shaull is the Chief Executive Officer and Head Coach of Unleashed CEO. **He helps entrepreneurs become "time-free CEOs"** of successful, scalable businesses. As a business owner, you'll learn how to regain time freedom, streamline your processes, and grow your team with his amazing philosophy and techniques.

SO YOU READ THIS BOOK. NOW WHAT?

Well, now it's up to you.

Over the course of 30+ chapters, we've provided you with the playbook to buy your own version of the American Dream. Like we said in the beginning, this isn't a get-rich-quick scheme. And it won't be easy.

But you know what else isn't easy? Living with the uncertainty of layoffs, dwindling savings accounts, or spending most of your life a slave to the time clock. The average lifespan in the United States is 77-80 years old. That gives you, what, 10-13 years post-retirement to "*live your best life?*"

Hell no.

Our sincere hope is that this book showed you that financial freedom **IS** attainable...*if you're willing to put in the necessary work.*

There's never been a better time to invest in yourself and your future. We raise our glass to you for taking this first important step; may it be the first of many.

A FINAL CALL TO ACTION:

We have one final call to action, and it's a biggie.

We've developed an app that's sort of like having an Investment Banker, Accountant, and Money Lender on speed dial.

Meet **Credit Banc.**

Specifically designed for business acquisitions, this one-stop-shop platform will monitor your personal and business credit and suggest personalized funding recommendations based on those scores. **Credit Banc** will also provide estimated business valuations along with real-life, time-tested, and proven strategies so you can analyze, fund, and grow your baby all in one place.

And because we always over-deliver, we're giving you, *our loyal readers,* discounted access to the app as a bonus for buying our book. Jumpstart your journey and get full use of **Credit Banc** over the next 14 days for just $1.

Go to www.creditbanc.io/dream and use code: DREAM.